October 6th, 2024

Gordon,

Here is a book that tells a lot
about Albania, and especially
about the Evangelical movement
among the people of Albania.
Thank you for hosting me at
Crestwood on this trip. I pray
and hope that God will continue
to grow our partnership for His
kingdom here and in Albania.

Tony

GERASIM KYRIAS

GERASIM KYRIAS

and the

Albanian National Awakening
1858–1894

Previously published as *A Sacred Task*

JOHN QUANRUD

Part of the 500/200 Albanian Protestant Commemorative Series
General Editor, David Hosaflook

Gerasim Kyrias and the Albanian National Awakening, 1858–1894

Originally published in 2002 as *A Sacred Task: the life of Gjerasim Qiriazi*

© John Quanrud, 2016

Published by the Institute for Albanian and Protestant Studies

ISBN 978-0-9934248-2-3

Publisher's Cataloging-in-Publication data

Names: Kuanrud, Xhon, 1959-, author.

Title: Gerasim Kyrias and the Albanian National Awakening, 1858–1894 / John Quanrud.

Series: The 500/200 Albanian Protestant Commemorative Series.

Description: "First published in English in 2002 as A Sacred Task by Authentic Lifestyle." | Includes bibliographical references and index. | Tirana, Albania: Institute for Albanian & Protestant Studies, 2016.

Identifiers: ISBN 978-0- 9934248-1- 6 (pbk.) | 978-0- 9934248-2- 3 (pbk.) | 978-0- 9934248-3- 0 (ebook)

Subjects: LCSH Qiriazi, Gjerasim, 1858-1894. | Authors, Albanian--19th century--Biography. | Educators--Albania--Biography. | Nationalism--Albania. | Albania--History--1878-1912. | BISAC BIOGRAPHY & AUTOBIOGRAPHY / Educators | BIOGRAPHY & AUTOBIOGRAPHY / Religious | HISTORY / Europe / Eastern | HISTORY / Middle East / Turkey & Ottoman Empire

Classification: LCC PG9621.Q53 Z75 2016 | DDC 949.6/501/92--dc23

Book and cover design: David Hosaflook and "Point"

Also available in Albanian as *Gjerasimi: predikues, iluminist, rilindës* (Tirana: Instituti për Studime Shqiptare dhe Protestante, 2016)

www.instituti.org

TABLE OF CONTENTS

For Lynne, Chloé and Nick

ACKNOWLEDGMENTS

THERE ARE MANY WHO have offered advice and counsel without whose kind help and generosity I could not have written this book. Special acknowledgment and thanks I give to the following; author of a comprehensive history of the Albanians and former missionary to Albania, the late Dr. Edwin Jacques, for his early encouragement and invaluable introduction to the subject; the late Gilbert Kyrias, Gerasim Kyrias's grandson, for the typewritten manuscript of Sevasti Kyrias's autobiography and a great meal; the late Alexander Dako, Sevasti's eldest son, for his warm friendship and valuable insights; Ameniel Bagdas, former Executive Secretary of the Turkish Bible Society in Istanbul for his patience and generosity; the late Dr. Prof. Hysni Myzyri for information concerning the development of Albanian societies during the late nineteenth century; Nicholas Smith, formerly of Cambridge University Library's Rare Books and Manuscripts Department, for helping me find a copy of Kyrias's book, *Captured by Brigands*; Alan Jesson, former librarian of the British and Foreign Bible Society's archives at Cambridge University, for his kind assistance; the staff of Houghton Library at Harvard University for their assistance with the papers of the American Board of Commissioners for Foreign Missions; Robert Walker for various translations from Greek and other languages; and, closer to home, my niece, Julie Anderson, who spent many weeks typing the contents of Alexander Thomson's letters into the word processor; my brother, Stephen Quanrud, for help in editing an early draft of this manuscript; and to my wife, Lynne, for patiently bearing with me during the long months of writing when the life of Gerasim Kyrias took over our lives.

ABBREVIATIONS

ABCFM   American Board of Commissioners
             for Foreign Missions

BFBS   The British and Foreign Bible Society

RTS   Religious Tract Society

TMAS   Turkish Mission Aid Society

VUSH   Vëllazëria Ungillore e Shqipërisë
             [The Albanian Evangelical Alliance]

Gerasim Kyrias, ca. 1884

Fear not, for I have redeemed you;
I have called you by name; you are mine.
When you pass through the waters
I will be with you;
and through the rivers,
they shall not overwhelm you;
when you walk through fire
you shall not be burned,
and the flame shall not consume you.
For I am the LORD your God,
The Holy one of Israel, your Saviour.

Isaiah 43:1–3

INTRODUCTION

WHEN NATO LAUNCHED ITS air offensive against Serbia in the spring of 1999, a great tide of Kosovar refugees began flooding into Albania, one of Europe's poorest nations. To their dismay they arrived to find that no one was ready for them. As their numbers continued to swell by the thousands, Albania's fragile infrastructure collapsed, leaving government and international humanitarian agency alike struggling to cope with a rapidly escalating crisis.

Suddenly, help came from an unexpected quarter. Through its network of over 120 churches across the country, the *Vëllazëria Ungjillore e Shqipërisë* or VUSH [Albania's Evangelical Alliance], with support from the *Albanian Encouragement Project* or AEP, quickly mobilised hundreds of volunteers to organise and run transit centres in every major town and city. Refugees were met, fed, registered and farmed out to families or camps in towns and surrounding areas. According to VUSH statistics, in the first two weeks of the crisis the evangelicals, who totalled less than half of a percent of the population, dealt with nearly 80 percent of the new arrivals. Throughout the months of the ordeal they continued to offer help and assistance wherever needed. It was a Herculean task which gained the churches the respect and gratitude of government officials from Shkodra to Gjirokaster.

In recognition of these efforts Albania's President, Rexhep Mejdani, wrote the following:

> I wish to acknowledge the Evangelical believers of Albania for the dedication and service rendered to tens of thousands of Kosovar refugees during one of the most difficult chapters in the history of our nation. Throughout the country these believers exemplified faith in action through their practical application of the Golden Rule, 'Do unto others as you would have them do unto you'. In this they have shown their determination to continue in the tradition of men like Gerasim Kyrias, who lived to serve his nation in the hope of making this world a better place.[1]

Many today are unaware of the existence of a Protestant community in Albania. Fewer still know the true story behind the distinguished Albanian national figure, Gerasim Kyrias. This book aims to redress the balance.

Political turmoil is nothing new to the Balkans. For the peoples of southern and central Europe, the end of the nineteenth century was also a period of great uncertainty. As the Ottoman Empire began its final decline, the threat of war pressed in on every side. Nations that had endured centuries of Turkish occupation struggled to free themselves from the Sultan's rule.

This was the critical period of Albania's *Rilindja* or National Awakening. It was during these years of political, social and economic upheaval that Gerasim Kyrias lived and worked. His achievements are all the more remarkable when viewed within the context of such realities.

'Heroes', wrote Gerasim's sister and co-worker, Sevasti, 'are those who sacrifice themselves for the sake of others, and not those who sacrifice others for their own sakes'.[2] Her brother epitomised this definition.

Though intellectually astute, Gerasim Kyrias was more than simply an educator or ideologue. He was a pioneer far ahead of his time, a man who 'set his hand to the plough and did not look back', even in the face of bitter and ruthless opposition. In a day when the majority of educated Albanians sought their fortunes far from Albania's troubled borders, Gerasim Kyrias chose to live and work among his people, enduring hardship at great personal risk.

His weapons were peaceful but powerful and his enemies feared him. He combined courage, intelligence and passion with the ability to communicate with words and, most threatening to those who opposed him, *Albanian* words. He travelled extensively, teaching and preaching in his mother tongue, bringing a message of hope and nurturing in his fellow countrymen a newly awakened sense of national identity. His songs, poems and sketches encouraged young and old alike to commit themselves to follow a higher way.

As a young man, Gerasim Kyrias dedicated himself to the gospel of Jesus Christ. His faith in God was profound, and served as the basis for his life and work. Although he died in 1894 at the age of thirty-five, the foundations he laid continued to impact future generations. Thousands of girls would be educated through the school he started with his sister, which ran, with some interruption, from 1891 until 1933 when King Zog issued a decree forbidding private education in Albania. The Protestant church in Kortcha, which grew out of his efforts, persevered through the decades despite severe repression, though only a handful of elderly believers survived to see the

fall of the communist system and the return of religious freedom in 1991. In 1992 the statutes of Kyrias's organisation, the
Vëllazëria Ungjillore, served as the basis of an application to the
government for today's VUSH. In January 1994, at celebrations
commemorating the 100th anniversary of Gerasim's death, the
Speaker of Parliament and leaders of Albania's traditional religious communities were among those present.

In 1983 a full-length feature film based on Gerasim Kyrias's
life was released in Albania entitled Mësonjtorja, or 'The School
House'. In 1987 he was awarded the title, 'Teacher of the
People', from Albania's communist dictatorship, and in 1992 he
received the prestigious 'Order of Freedom — First Class', from
the newly elected democratic government.

Until recently, however, two factors have combined to
hinder objective research concerning Gerasim Kyrias. First and
foremost was the restrictive environment created by the former
communist regime under which Albanian historians laboured
for nearly 50 years. To ensure their historical interpretations did
not transgress the narrow confines of Marxist-Leninist ideology,
state censors strictly controlled every word that was published.
In the years following the Second World War, Gerasim Kyrias
was viewed with suspicion for his overtly religious activity and
foreign affiliations. Though decades had passed since his death,
Gerasim's sisters and their families suffered persecution. In
1947 Sevasti's two sons were falsely accused as spies and thrown
into prison. George, her youngest and a much-valued medical
doctor, was unable to withstand the torture and confinement
and hung himself there in 1949. Within months Sevasti, the
indefatigable champion of women's education in Albania, had
died of a broken heart.

It was not until the early 1960s that a change took place in the attitude of Albania's communist leadership. This change is largely owed to the intervention of a flamboyant Albanian historian, Skender Luarasi, son of Gerasim's close friend and associate, Petro Nini Luarasi. Skender Luarasi greatly admired the Kyrias family and in particular the sisters Sevasti and Paraskevi for what he deemed as their inestimable contribution to Albania and the Albanian people.

Of all the Kyrias family it is the two sisters who are best known today. Articles and papers continue to be written about them.[3] There were, until recently, a number of elderly women still in Albania, often conversant in English and French, who attended their school, and remembered them with great respect and admiration. In Kosova a society bears their name, *Motrat Kyrias* (The Kyrias Sisters Society), which has been one of the most active forces in promoting Albanian education and the eradication of illiteracy there.

In her memoirs, Sevasti made it clear that the vision and inspiration behind her work came from her beloved brother, Gerasim.

As part of his plan to shift the communist regime's aggressive stance against the Kyrias family, Skender Luarasi wrote a short biography entitled *Gerasim Kyrias, Jeta dhe Vepra* (Gerasim Kyrias, His Life and Writings). It is based primarily on interviews with Gerasim's youngest sister, Paraskevi, then eighty years of age, and Sevasti's memoirs, much of which were written from memory in the 1930s. Luarasi's book, without footnotes or bibliography, was approved by the censors and published in Tirana in 1962. In it the basic outline of Kyrias's life is given, while the man himself undergoes something of a baptism of socialist fire. Luarasi resolved the sensitive problem of Kyrias's

religious convictions and foreign contacts by alleging the young
patriot cleverly duped his Protestant missionary associates with
a feigned conversion to gain their favour and thus the political
clout of their respective governments. This act of duplicity,
he argues, enabled Kyrias to realise his true aims, which were
purely nationalistic and secular. Kyrias's writings were also carefully edited of any material the communist censors might find
unsuitable. And thus, in post-war communist Albania, seventy
years after his death, Gerasim Kyrias was granted a place among
Albania's plethora of national heroes and his youngest sister,
Paraskevi, began to receive a small state pension.

Subsequent works concerning Kyrias have largely repeated
Luarasi's conclusions, as well as this biography's factual errors,
from the wrong year of birth to more serious mistakes such as
the assertion he died a bachelor when in fact he was married
and fathered a child.[4]

The second problem confronting Albanian historians writing
about Gerasim Kyrias has to do with the limited amount of
source material available in their country. The overwhelming
majority of letters and documents written by him, to him, or
about him — of which literally hundreds have survived — lie
beyond Albania's borders in the archives, libraries and offices of
those societies and organizations with which he was associated.
Access to these materials is fundamental in establishing who he
really was and what he stood for.

I was first introduced to the subject in 1987, soon after I began
studying Albanian in Kosova's capital, Prishtina. My language
tutor at the time, an Albanian student at Prishtina University
named Bexhet, read me a poem he had written about the Kyrias
family and their role in the monumental Congress of Monastir

in 1908, when the potentially divisive issue of which alphabet to use for writing Albanian was finally decided. Though I struggled to understand the words, Bexhet's obvious passion for this family and their achievements took me by surprise. Never before had I seen a student choke back tears while speaking of historical figures long dead. It was my first exposure to the incredible power history holds over the lives of the peoples of the Balkans.

The fact I was in Kosova at all dated back to a turning point in my own life. Several years earlier I had read an article about Albania, a country of which, until then, I had known nothing. It spoke of Albania's xenophobic communist dictatorship and the brutal suppression of all religious belief and practice; how in 1967 over two thousand mosques and churches had been destroyed or converted to other uses and of the ensuing purge against both Christian and Muslim religious leaders, many of whom were imprisoned, exiled or shot. 'The Albanian people do not believe in God', boasted the authorities, 'because God does not believe in the Albanian people.' Astonished by such arrogance and intolerance, by the time I finished reading the article something inside me had changed. I felt certain that one day I would go to Albania.

A few weeks after reading Bexhet's poem, a friend sent me a copy of an old Albanian hymnal including many hymns written by Gerasim and his siblings.[5] When I asked Bexhet if the Kyriases of the hymnal and the Kyriases of his poem might be the same family, he immediately refuted the idea. In his mind it was impossible for such national heroes to have been Protestant Christians. A few days later he cheerfully produced a copy of Luarasi's biography, which seemingly explained the existence of the hymnal. Suspicious of Luarasi's conclusions, I decided to begin my own search to uncover what I could about Gerasim Kyrias.

This book is the result of that search which, over a period of several years, took me from Kosova to Albania, the Republic of Macedonia, Greece, Turkey, England, and America; at times seated in the comfortable environs of organised archives and libraries with convenient document lists and order forms, but more often to office storage rooms or the cellars and attics of descendants in distant lands.

The most significant discovery by far came in Istanbul, in the back rooms of the former offices of the British and Foreign Bible Society, which, at the time of my visit, were home to the Turkish Bible Society. The director kindly allowed me to rummage there for a day in 1989, though he was certain I had made a wasted journey. Undeterred, I spent several hours sifting through books and papers thick with dust, at one point falling from the rafters and crashing to the floor, bringing a distraught director rushing in, fearing the worst. Then, just as I was about to give up, everything changed. Hidden away on a metal shelf at the back of a storage room stood a number of packages wrapped in plain, brown paper. To my amazement I found inside numerous letter-books belonging to Alexander Thomson, head of the Bible Society's work in the Ottoman Empire from 1860–96. Thomson was Gerasim's boss and mentor during the last ten years of his life when he worked for the British and Foreign Bible Society. Between the worn covers of these old volumes were, incredibly, copies pressed on wafer thin sheets of thousands of Thomson's letters from the 1870s until his retirement in 1896. Other materials and correspondence were also scattered throughout. I had struck gold.

From these and other primary sources, many of which are used here for the first time, a complete picture of Kyrias's life and work emerges. They reveal a stirring example of the power of the human spirit to persevere despite innumerable dangers and difficulties in the determination to turn a dream into reality. They also answer the question of Kyrias's faith, for we find he was not merely a believer, but a man whose faith in God served as the very catalyst that spurred him into action, inspiring and motivating him to pursue the national cause. It was Gerasim's conviction that the message of the gospel, which had so dramatically affected his own life, held the key to the nation's future prosperity.

Furthermore, Kyrias's story offers a unique glimpse into the present-day tensions in the Balkans, by allowing us to see, first hand as it were, how the rival nations there have dealt with one another in the past as they sought to secure their own national and political interests.

It is my hope that this work will bring new insight into the life of a man who gave everything to serve his nation and for it paid the ultimate price.

To simplify things for the reader, I have standardised the spelling of proper names and titles in the source materials, preferring the standard English spellings. For example, the English version of the Albanian town of Kortcha appears in source manuscripts as *Koritza*, *Gyjördje*, or *Korça* (the Albanian spelling), but "Kortcha" is used here. Likewise, the present-day city of Bitola, in the Republic of Macedonia, was known as Monastir in Kyrias's day, and is referred to as Monastir in this book.

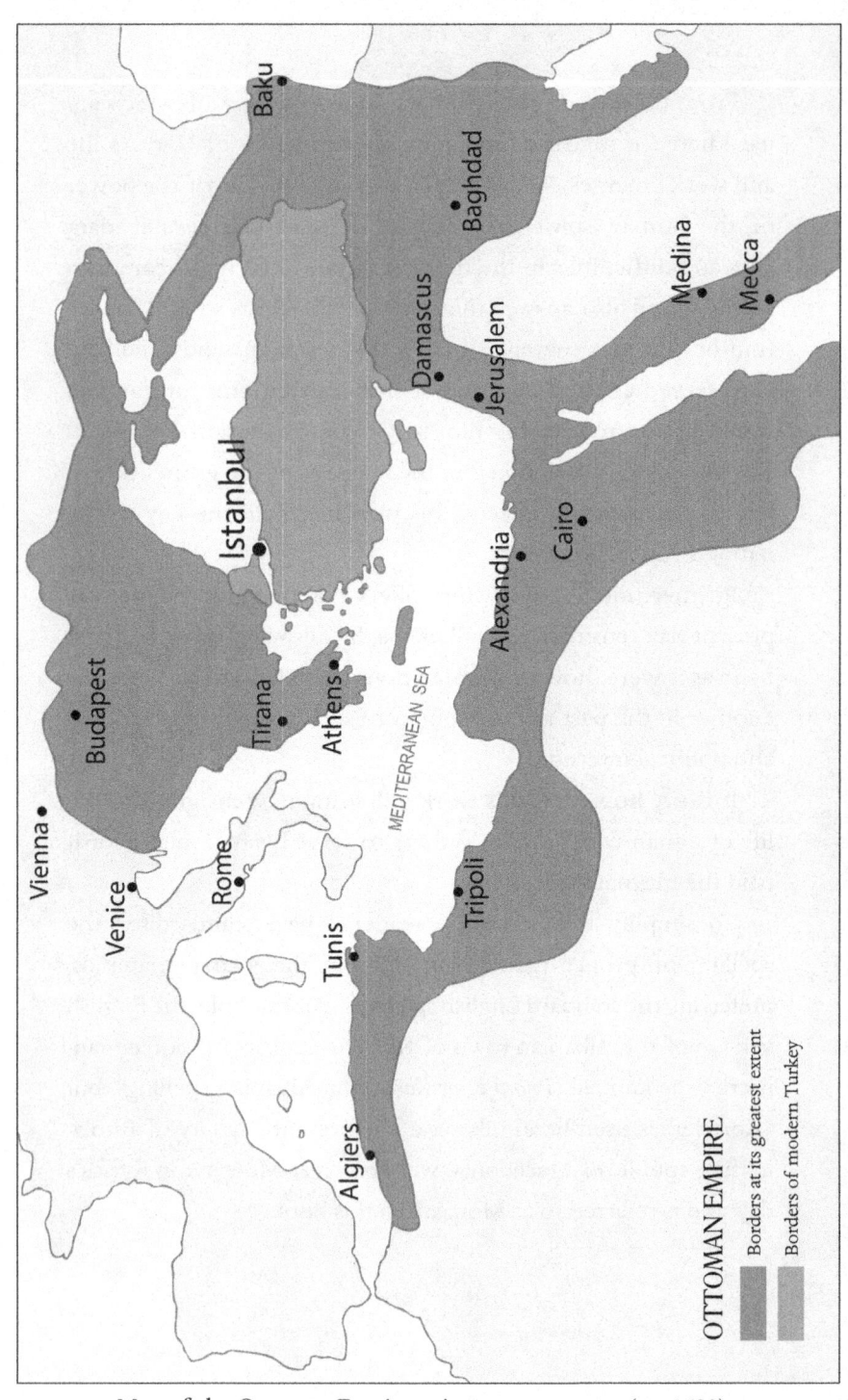

Map of the Ottoman Empire at its greatest extent (ca. 1683)

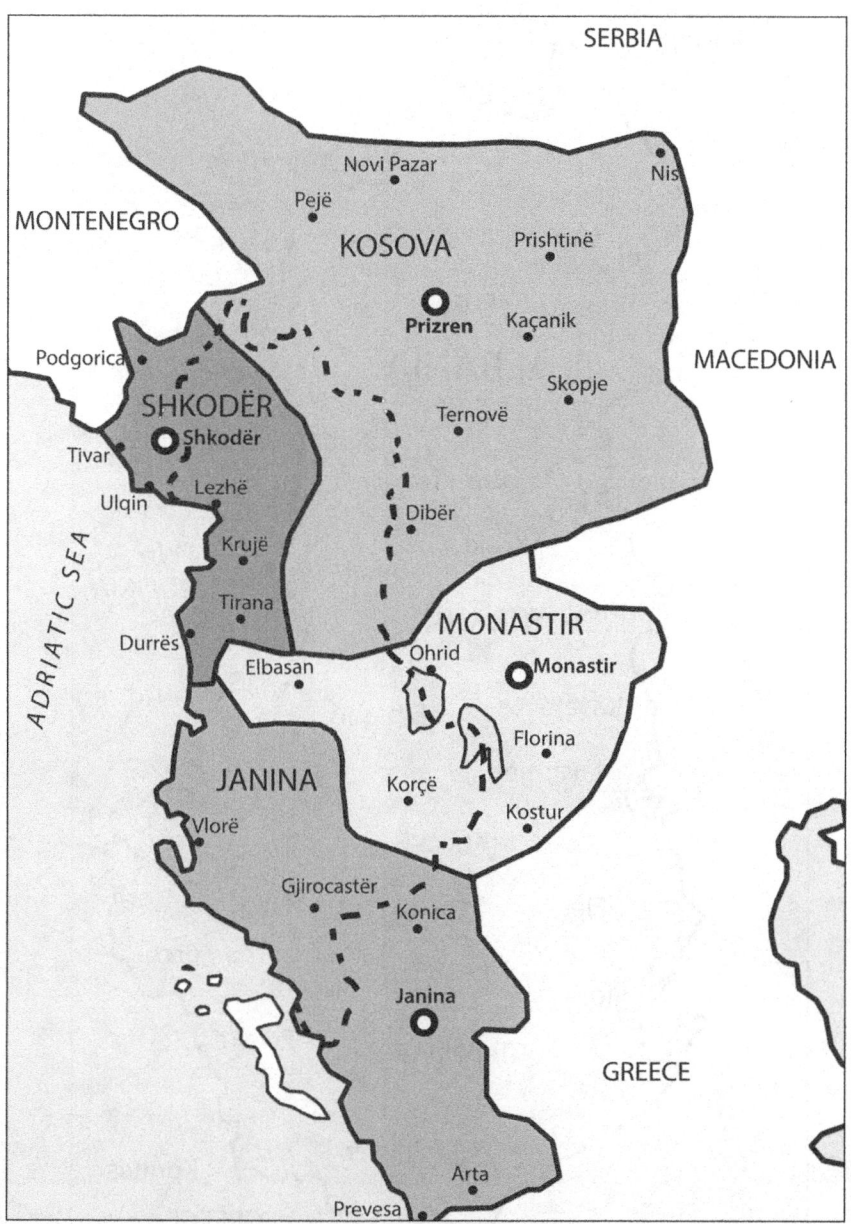

Albania (its modern borders in outline) and the four Ottoman vilayets encompassing Albanian territories at the end of the 19th century.

Map of Modern Albania

CHAPTER 1

BEGINNINGS

ALBANIA. KNOWN FOR GENERATIONS to the tribes inhabiting its rugged terrain as *Shqipëria*, 'the Land of the Eagle', and to the outside world in more recent times as a bastion of Marxist-Leninism and 'The World's First Atheist State', modern Albania lies in the heart of the Balkans, sharing its borders with Montenegro, Kosova, the Republic of Macedonia, and Greece. Its people, the *Shqiptarë*, or 'Sons of the Eagle', have, over the centuries, seen the armies of great empires invade, conquer, rule and disappear. Nonetheless, her fiercely independent clans were able to maintain high levels of autonomy from their impenetrable mountain strongholds, defending themselves against Roman, Byzantine, Slavic, Norman, Venetian, Turkish and other invaders. None was ever able to completely subdue or assimilate the indigenous population, but the longer the period of occupation, the greater the mark left on local culture and beliefs.

During the fourteenth century the Ottoman star was in its ascendancy. The Muslim Turks, having conquered most of the Byzantine lands of the East, looked westward to the Christian lands of Europe. A coalition of Hungarians, Bulgarians,

Romanians, Poles, Serbs and Albanians lost the decisive Battle
of Kosova in 1389 and the Sultan's armies continued their con-
quests to the north and west. Later the Albanians, under the
leadership of their national hero, Gjergj Kastrioti or Skanderbeg,
with his incredible genius for guerrilla warfare, repelled succes-
sive Turkish onslaughts until his death in 1468. Then, with none
to lead them, kingdom after kingdom capitulated before the
advancing foe. By the beginning of the sixteenth century all of
Albania had succumbed to Ottoman rule.

At its peak, the Ottoman Empire stretched from what is
today Croatia and Hungary in the northwest, southward along
the Adriatic coast to Greece and North Africa, across to the
Caspian Sea and the Persian Gulf in the East. In addition to the
Turkic peoples, the Sultan's subjects also included Austrians,
Hungarians, Croats, Serbs, Bosnians, Bulgars, Romanians,
Montenegrins, Albanians, Greeks, Vlachs, Russians, Africans,
Egyptians, Jews, Lebanese, Armenians, Kurds, Persians, Arabs,
and many more.

To administrate their vast domain, the Sultans eventually
divided the Empire into provinces called *vilayets*. Each vilayet
was overseen by a governor known as a *vali*. The valis were
responsible to the Sultan and his *Grand Vizier* or Prime Minister,
who presided over the cabinet, called the *Sublime Porte*, which
became 'the principal executive and administrative department
of the government'.[1]

Numerous officials administered the vilayets but the following descriptions will suffice for the purpose of our story. *Pashas*
were high-ranking military or political officials. *Mutasarrifs*
served as district (*sanjak*) administrators with *kaymakams* under
them. There were also *muhtars*, who were village elders or

mayors. The local police force was made up of gendarmes called *zaptiehs*, who were generally poorly educated and poorly paid. Feudal landowners were called *beys*, with such titles bestowed in return for special or distinguished service. Beys were obliged to provide military service to the state when the need arose. Only Muslims could become beys.

From the beginning of the nineteenth century, demands for autonomy had grown among the various nations of the Ottoman Empire. In the 1820s, the Greeks fought and won a war of independence and, throughout the period, Russian and Slavic alliances made advances from the north and northwest of the Empire. As a result of the Crimean War (1853–6), a land dispute in which England and France supported Turkey against Russia, the Sultan agreed to new concessions including equality and reform for all his subjects, Christian and Muslim alike.

Such unrest was costly and took its toll on government reserves. Facing crisis upon crisis, the stability of the Ottoman Empire waned. Turkey's neighbours and the Great Powers of Europe, in particular France, Austro-Hungary and England, vied for possession or political influence as they watched and waited for its inevitable demise.

In the westernmost corner of this Empire lived the Albanians, divided among the vilayets of Shkodra, Yanina, Monastir, and Skopje. In general, the Albanians had not fared well under Ottoman rule. Mismanagement, neglect, and high taxes had led to widespread poverty and suffering. Poor communications, few roads and even fewer bridges prevented economic development and made Albania virtually inaccessible to the foreign visitor, though some dared to venture within her borders. The most articulate of these, England's illustrious Lord Byron, immortalised his impressions of her people in the epic poem, *Childe Harold's Pilgrimage*. He wrote:

> Fierce are Albania's children, yet they lack
> Not virtues; were those virtues more mature
> Where is the foe that ever saw their back?
> Who can so well the toils of war endure?
> Their native fastnesses nor more secure;
> Then in doubtful time of troublous need.
> Their wrath, how deadly! But their friendship sure.
> When gratitude or valor bids them bleed,
> Unshaken, rushing on where'er their chief may lead.[2]

The city of Monastir, capital of Monastir Vilayet and home to the Kyrias family, served as both an economic centre and a military base. Strategically situated on the main highway between Albania and the East, many Albanians frequented the inns of Monastir while conducting trade and other activities in the city. Its population was a jumble of nationalities. Each day a colourful display of costumes and cultures paraded through the marketplace. Shopkeepers bartered in any number of languages, at times using several in the same breath.

Though the 'Macedonian Crisis' did not explode into international headlines until 1903, signs of unrest preceded it by decades. Bands of brigands raided unsuspecting villages or swooped down on travellers, making life even more miserable for the general populace. Justice was a rare commodity, with officials meting out arbitrary sentences when a bribe was not forthcoming.

At other times it was the Turkish military that inflicted suffering. It was not uncommon for Christian villages, at odds with the authorities, to be burned and razed, the survivors forced to seek refuge in other parts of the Empire.

Such was the fate of Peras, a village in the district of Kolonia in southern Albania, in the early 1800s. The families took what possessions they could and fled eastward, some settling in Ternova, a village in the foothills a few miles outside of Monastir. One of the children, Kyrias Michael, made his living from carpentry, and taught the trade to his sons.

His youngest son, Dhimiter, married Maria and together they raised ten children, seven sons and three daughters. Dhimiter owned a carpentry shop in Monastir where he stayed during the week.

Their third child, Gerasim Dhimiter Kyrias, was born on 18 October 1858. Though the family was by language and culture Albanian, they belonged to the Greek Orthodox Church and Gerasim would have been baptised shortly after his birth.

From the earliest days of the Empire the Sultans made use of the existing religious structures to help administrate their vast domain. Laws were enacted granting the various religious communities specific rights and privileges under what became known as the *millet system* (*millet*, Turk., people or nation). The religious millets were allowed to practice their religion and retain their properties if they agreed to submit to the Sultan's temporal authority. The religious millet leaders also carried civil authority in certain instances. From birth every Ottoman citizen belonged to his or her family's religious millet. The millets eventually organised their own schools, an important concession which ensured the continuity of national and religious identity from one generation to the next.

As a young boy Gerasim was enrolled at the local Greek school, for there were no Albanian schools at that time. Under the millet system the Albanians were not recognised as a separate nationality. Roman Catholic Albanians were numbered along with Venetians, Croats or Austro-Hungarians, Muslim Albanians as Turks, and Orthodox Albanians as Greeks or Slavs. Gerasim's early education was entirely in the Greek language with a particular emphasis on Greek culture and history.

Gerasim was still very young when his father sold their house in Ternova and moved to Monastir. In her memoirs Gerasim's younger sister, Sevasti, portrays a picture of pleasant family life. She recalled how their father would gather the children and recite stories in the ancient Albanian oral tradition of countless generations before him.

> Through with the dinner, the basin and pitcher was brought in for washing hands and mouth. The sofra, [a low, round table from which meals were eaten] was cleared, father called for his *narghileh*, a tobacco pipe with a long flexible tube for steam to pass through a vessel containing water, often rose water...
>
> When through with the narghileh, father used to tell us thrilling stories of our ancestors or Albanian heroes, which were imparted so vividly as to keep us all spellbound. Father's patriotic feelings did not fail to inspire us with that spirit of his which grew with the years and made all his children good patriots who gave heart and soul to the cause of Albania.[3]

From contact with friends and simply from growing up in Monastir, Gerasim was fluent in several languages. Apart from his native Albanian and the Greek he learned at school, he also knew Wallachian, a Romanian dialect spoken by the Vlachs who were descendants of Latin tribes, Bulgarian, as the Slavic dialect of Macedonia was then known, and Turkish, the language of the Empire.

We know little else of his early childhood except that he was taken from school at the age of thirteen and apprenticed to a local shoemaker to help support his family. Working in a small shop in the market, Gerasim proved a competent craftsman. And such he would have remained, a simple cobbler faithfully plying his trade but for the arrival in Monastir of unexpected neighbours on the day he turned fifteen.

CHAPTER 2

WINDS OF REVIVAL

ON 5 OCTOBER 1872, three new Protestant missionaries, John Baird, George Marsh and John House, set sail from New York harbour headed for European Turkey. In November they arrived in the city of Eski Zagra (today Stara Zagora in southern Bulgaria), where they 'engaged in the study of the language, while becoming acquainted with, and aiding as they could, in the details of missionary work'.[1] Baird, aged twenty-six, had graduated from Chicago Seminary only a few months before leaving America.

In the United States he had met twenty-three-year-old Ellen Richardson, the daughter of a missionary to Turkey. Having finished her studies, Ellen was about to return to her family in Bursa. Baird later visited her at her parent's home, a romance ensued, and they were married on 17 September 1873.

At this time another young couple were making final preparations for missionary life in Turkey. Edward Jenney and Kate Thrall were married on 12 August 1873. Two weeks later they sailed from New York Harbour. Jenney, aged twenty-eight, was a veteran of the American Civil War. He graduated from Knox College in Illinois in 1870 and Andover Seminary in

Massachusetts in 1873. His wife Kate, aged twenty-five, was also a graduate of Knox College in one of the first classes to admit women to full academic standing.

Brimming with youthful energy and optimism, these two couples, the Bairds and the Jenneys, would soon join forces to establish the first Protestant mission outpost in Macedonia.

They were sent under the auspices of the American Board of Commissioners for Foreign Missions, established in 1810 to give support to an enthusiastic group of students in their missionary endeavours. The American Board, as it became known, publicised the dramatic stories of these early pioneers, many of whom laid down their lives for the sake of the gospel. Their testimonies ignited a fervour for missions among the American churches resulting in thousands more giving themselves to missionary service.

Ottoman Turkey saw the arrival of the first Protestant missionaries early in the nineteenth century. From Constantinople (Istanbul) and Smyrna (Izmir) mission stations were eventually established across the Empire, even in the remotest regions. The concessions made by the Sultan in the form of his famous *Hatt-i-Hümayun* in 1856 following the Crimean War allowed greater freedom for missionary activity. In 1872, Bible House was built. A four-storey limestone building that still stands in the heart of Istanbul, it housed the central headquarters of the American Board's Turkish Mission, the American Bible Society and the offices of the British and Foreign Bible Society.

Alongside evangelistic activity, the missionaries were also strongly committed to education. The establishment of schools and colleges formed an integral part of the work, a fact clearly evidenced by the Turkish Mission. Cyrus Hamlin, a former

American Board missionary, founded the renowned Robert College at Constantinople. Four other colleges — including Constantinople College for Women where Gerasim's younger sisters, Sevasti and Paraskevi, later earned their diplomas — were also the results of missionaries' labours.

Statistics for Protestant work in Ottoman Turkey including Egypt for 1894 show 892 mission schools teaching 23,027 children. The same report put the total number of foreign missionaries in the Ottoman Empire at that time at 485, with 1,817 native labourers, 202 organised churches, 21,312 communicants, and 84,000 Protestants.[2]

This extensive labour left its mark. In a paper given at the American Farm School of Thessaloniki in 1910, British journalist, editor, and founder of the noted periodical *Review of Reviews*, William T. Stead, who was to perish on the ill-fated *Titanic* two years later on his way to New York to address an international conference on world peace and international arbitration, referred to the missionaries when he said:

> It is not too much to say that the only infusion of western civilization in the eastern races has come not from Great Britain or Germany, but from America. Great Britain, absorbed in diplomatic, naval and military affairs, has spent untold millions of dollars in propping up the political system established in the East. The American government on the other hand spends nothing and has accomplished nothing. But private American citizens subscribing out of their own pockets sums that in 50 years might have equaled the amount spent to build one modern ironclad, have left in every province of the Ottoman empire the imprint of their intelligence and character.[3]

By 1873, the Mission's work in Turkey had grown so large that
the arrival of new missionaries in Monastir received little attention. The Annual Report of the American Board for that year
included the following announcement, as if in passing:

> [The new station at *Monastir* was first occupied by Messrs.
> Baird and Jenney and their wives, and Mr. Marsh in
> October, 1873.]

The journey there had been arduous. Monastir was not yet ser-
viced by rail, so they travelled on simple carts over rough roads
and slept in bug-infested *khans* or inns along the way. When the
weary missionaries finally arrived in Monastir on 18 October
1873, they found it a city like none they had ever seen. One E. B.
Haskell visited Monastir some twenty years later and described
his first impressions:

> It is now, as it was then a Turkish city with white minarets
> and crooked streets full of dogs, in which the law com-
> pelled you to carry a lighted lantern two hours after sun-
> set, even though the moon be shining bright enough to
> read by. It has been a strong military station, and a Babel
> of tongues and a circus of costumes beyond imagination.
> Barnum is a puny sideshow to what we see every market
> day. The 40,000 inhabitants consist of Turks, Bulgarians,
> Wallachians, Greeks, Albanians, Jews, Gypsies and 'scat-
> tering'… The official language is Turkish, the language of
> trade, Bulgarian, and the 'upper class' language French.
> For the highest efficiency here a missionary should learn
> the above three beside his own.[4]

Monastir was chosen 'because of its healthfulness, and because it is not only the governmental center, but also, to some extent, a commercial center'. The missionaries rented houses and set about the task of establishing themselves in their new city. During the first year much time was given to studying the Bulgarian language. They soon began a service conducted by a 'native worker' in Bulgarian, the attendance of which gradually increased to sixty. But as there was not sufficient work for them all, Marsh was later reassigned to Eski Zagra.

The arrival of the missionaries did not pass unnoticed by the people of Monastir. 'The Americans' became a favourite topic in the market place and teahouses, though in time the excitement waned. Jenney explains:

> ... the curiosity which was awakened by our arrival in Monastir two years ago this coming fall, has now settled into a calm and we trust an earnest enquiry for the truth. The hasty, thoughtless, polite assertion, 'You are right, and we are wrong'; has in many instances changed to the inquiry; 'What is truth?' The crowds who at first thronged our chapel room, found the word too pointed, too destructive to favorite plans in life, and little by little left us; but we rejoice more in the present few, who, Bible in hand, study the Word of God.[5]

They held religious services, conversed at large with the people and distributed religious tracts and literature throughout the town and surrounding villages. Through them the winds of the Reformation began to blow into Macedonia.

The missionaries longed to see an intensification of personal religious life. Their message, based on the Apostles' teachings, offered a restored relationship with God through the forgiveness of sins by Christ's sacrificial death on the cross. Faith was a choice of the individual and they opposed merely formal, conventional, external, and nominal forms of Christianity. Special emphasis was given to the doctrines of original sin, salvation by faith, and sanctification through the work of the Holy Spirit.

Jenney soon became known as 'the good American'. His reports from those early days reveal the earnestness with which they laboured:

> For some time I have been visiting the shopkeepers in the market, sometimes making three or four calls in an hour and again spending three or four hours in one shop. I tried at first to gain attention by immediately entering into conversation, but to no purpose; for as soon as it was discovered that I did not wish to buy, I could see impatience, and a desire that I should leave. I therefore took a satchel filled with our smaller books and with my pockets filled with tracts, I started out. As I expected, the rich looked down upon me with contempt, and I could see that many were laughing at me for having become a bookseller. The first day, as bookseller, in about seven hours, I visited twenty-five shops. In several of these I held conversation, but in others I was as kindly as possible, told by the proprietor that his men could not work so well when I was talking; hence I soon left, but I was often encouraged by the evident influence of the Spirit on the hearts of men.
>
> In another shop, (the proprietor of which is a regular attendant upon our services, is intellectually convinced of the truth and argues for 'Evangelical belief', as they term our faith), I talked for four hours at once. The little shop

and its door were almost constantly crowded, though the
crowd did not remain the same for fifteen minutes at a
time. I never have met so much opposition in Monastir as
upon that day. But the truth took hold of them. Two or
three would oppose for a time, then, when met by unan-
swerable arguments, they would go away as if fleeing from
a serpent, but would return in a few minutes. At last one
man, who had been informed what my arguments were,
came and in a loud voice pronounced all a lie. He swung
his arm so that I was in danger of receiving a blow. I took
his hand in both of mine, and soon he was as calm as any.
For half an hour I argued with him. At last he acknowl-
edged that he knew of no reply, and declared plainly that
if I was right, as I seemed to be, the faith of the Bulgarian
church was false. As I urged them to search truth, and
prepare in Christ's own way for heaven, those once bitter
opposers remained quiet, and appeared really serious.[6]

The Civil War veteran signed his letter, 'Yours on the skirmish
line'. Gradually through their efforts, more and more people
began, in Jenney's words, 'to come into the light'. Stories of
men like George, a silversmith of Monastir, became known
throughout the city. Though ridiculed by friends and family for
having 'changed religions', George held firmly to his convictions. Jenney wrote the following memoir in August 1876:

> Two years ago someone spoke very strongly against the
> Protestants here, when [George's] wife said, 'I am glad, for
> my part, that they have come. Before they came George
> used to spend his Sabbaths in the liquor saloons and only
> came home for a few minutes to abuse me and to return
> to drink more. Now he does not drink and when not in

meetings he reads the Testament to me, and I have him
all day to myself.'

For a year and a half he seemed to be curious to know
our faith, but the truth did not seem to take hold of him,
so that we feared he would not come out for Christ. But
for a year and a half he has been fearless in presenting the
Word to his neighbors, and has been known by all as a
Protestant. I have held as many conversations in his shop
as I deemed best, and he always translated into Greek and
Wallachian according to the audience.

For more than a year he has been ill with the consumption. Little by little the disease has brought him down and
for three months he was confined to his room. The last
three weeks of this sickness I visited him daily and he
always wished, as he said 'more instruction in the Christian
life.' The tears would come as I spoke of the love of Jesus
to fallen man, and he always wept as he referred to his past
life of sin. When the priest came to pray over him he told
him to leave, adding, 'I cannot understand you and you do
not understand yourself.' Oct[ober] 24th he went home.[7]

The Protestant movement in Monastir was gaining momen-
tum. In 1876, a young man named Nikola became the first to
seek membership in the Protestant church. It would be a costly
decision.

The Greek Orthodox leaders had threatened to excom-
municate the families of any who attended Protestant meetings. They refused to baptise, marry, or bury anyone whose
relatives associated with the Protestants. Terrified by the social
ramifications of such extreme measures, the families brought
intense pressure to bear on any of their own who disobeyed
the ban. Concerned that Nikola might be unprepared for such

opposition, Jenney recommended he put off the decision for a time to 'test his love for Jesus by works'. Thus Nikola proved himself an effective missionary:

> From that time he has brought from one to five of his companions to each service, most of them being strangers to us. One of these, for three months, has been in regular attendance, and for two months has had a desire to lead a new life and join us. Both of these young men come to me every week to receive instruction, as they are very ignorant in religious matters. We hope to see them earnest Christians.[8]

It was agreed that Nikola and his companion, Demeter, be publicly examined for membership on Sunday, 31 December 1876. They were the first residents of Monastir to join the Protestant communion. The event aroused a great deal of 'excitement:'

> A few minutes before examination [Nikola and Demeter] called upon me and I discovered that their mothers had not been informed as to the step they were about to take. I therefore advised them as dutiful sons to go home and tell them adding, 'I do not require it.' They sat in silence for a few minutes. At last Demeter said 'God sent us here to learn our duty.' They went home immediately and although late to the service were happy in that they brought their mothers with them. This was a heavy cross for them since they expected trouble, for their mothers had strongly withstood and threatened them.
>   When they promised to try to live according to the gospel, one mother spoke up saying 'if you partake of the

sacrament the curse of your mother falls upon you. We
shall die as our parents did, and wish our children to do
likewise.' The whole affair was very exciting and made
our hearts bleed for these poor deluded women. Lying
neighbors are bringing all manner of accusation against
us and these young men, in order to make the mothers
more bitter opposers.

Neighbors and priests tried it but the only result was
that the strongest opponent exclaimed, after he had failed
to meet their arguments, 'there is no God'.[9]

Nikola and Demeter became 'valuable workers in the vineyard'.
They visited the missionaries regularly to learn more about
Christian faith. Friends were intrigued by their talk of spiritual
matters. Some mocked them but others showed a sincere interest in the Bible and numbers at the meetings grew. By the spring
of 1877, Monastir had begun to experience the first signs of a
religious revival. Here, Gerasim would be forever changed.

The missionaries rented a house behind the Kyrias's and
the family was well aware of their activities. Initially Gerasim
shared in the many prejudices held against them and their principles, and on occasion would go with his companions to dis-
rupt the meetings.[10] Then, in 1877, he came under the influence
of Nikola and Demeter. A gradual change began to take place
in the young shoemaker.

During this time Sevasti fell ill with malarial fever. One day
Jenney, the 'good American', passed the house and heard the
sound of her crying through the open kitchen window. He
stopped to inquire about her and began visiting daily, bringing
small gifts and medicines until she recovered. Touched by this
act of kindness, as Gerasim observed Jenney and Baird, he soon

became 'so impressed by their blameless life, the uprightness and kindness of the missionaries, and their observance of the Lord's Day, that he began to think seriously of what they said. He bought a Greek New Testament, and began to read it regularly, and was led to see himself a sinner, and to seek redemption in Jesus Christ.'[11] His reading of the scriptures became a source of deep satisfaction.

Caught up in the joy of his newfound faith, Gerasim participated eagerly in the special meetings held each week by the missionaries. 'All the objections to the truth', wrote Jenney, 'and all the arguments they may have used in supporting their faith, have been considered, and they are shown when they failed, and aided by proof texts to make their arguments stronger.'[12] Gerasim developed a passion for the gospel and longed to preach its message. It was this passion that would motivate him for the rest of his life.

Gerasim soon made a positive impression on the missionaries. On 2 August 1877, Baird wrote:

> I think in less than two weeks we shall examine three persons, a man and his wife, and a young man for admission to communion. When they publicly profess Christ there may be some persecution but not very fierce. But we don't think persecution the worst thing that can befall us — it is better than indifference any day. The young man is an Arnavut (Albanian) and may some day make a good preacher. He has a good mind and seems consecrated.

Gerasim's decision to join the Protestant church was not taken lightly by his family who, fearing retribution from the Greek

Orthodox clergy, tried to dissuade him. But even at eighteen, Gerasim displayed an acute sense of conscience and conviction, which was to mark him in later years. He allowed neither convention, tradition, nor even personal safety to stand in the way of what he perceived as truth or duty. In the teachings of the New Testament Gerasim had encountered a power that changed his life. Thus on 19 August 1877, he was examined and accepted into the Protestant church of Monastir, 'amid severe persecution from his parents and relatives, which', he later explained, 'greatly strengthened his faith, and matured his character.'[13] Eventually his family came to accept and even support him. Over the years several brothers and sisters would follow. It was a pivotal decision that deeply affected him personally and started him, unwittingly, on a path that would lead him to the forefront of the Albanian national movement.

For this to happen, however, he would require further training. In their commitment to education, the missionaries organised 'station classes' to prepare potential students for further study at one of the Mission's secondary schools. Such classes had been attempted at Monastir in previous years, without result. Now, with such promising candidates as Gerasim and Nikola, the missionaries at Monastir decided to make another attempt. Baird spoke with the boys.

Overjoyed by this unexpected opportunity to resume his studies, Gerasim sought his father's permission. Dhimiter Kyrias, though reluctant at first, eventually gave his consent and, early in December 1877, classes began. Nikola's friend, Demeter, soon joined them. Each day after work the three resumed their lessons. Baird's correspondence outlines their progress.

Monastir

December 6, 1877

Here the Lord's work is in a very hopeful condition. The young converts seem to be growing in grace, knowledge and devotion. They have only the kindest of feelings for us. With Mr. Jenney's consent before he left I have begun a station class of two, one a Vlach and the other Arnavut (Albanian) both earnest and promising young men who have some education in Greek and know that language quite well. They speak Bulgarian fairly and all their studies are in the latter language. I think they can be well prepared to enter the Theo[logical] Sem[inary] next fall with the class that then enters. They both have trades and are *first class* workmen in them.

Monastir,

January 22, 1878

A few days after Mr. Jenney's departure I spoke to two young men (communicants) and they were delighted at the opportunity. I advised them to continue working at their trades for the present at least which they are doing. But as times are very slack they have time enough to learn one good lesson per day. As soon now as we can get the necessary text books they will have two lessons per day. A day or so after recitations began a third young man joined it. These young men support themselves at present and will no doubt continue to till they go to Samokov. As they are bright and earnest I think they will be prepared to enter Samokov next Sept[ember] if there is nothing unexpected to hinder them. They have gone over the fundamentals three or more years ago, but in the Greek language.

Monastir,
April 5, 1878
The helper has them in Bulg[arian] grammar and Jones'
Catechism, while I have them in Arithmetic and Algebra.
In the latter study the helper himself is a student.
Fortunately we have good text books. The Arith[metic]
is quite as good as any I have studied in America and the
algebra is a translation of Greenleaf's. I hope to finish up
arithmetic in 6 weeks and then put them into anatomy
and physiology.

Monastir,
June 30, 1878
Early in Dec[ember] a station class of three young men,
communicants, was formed, taught by missionaries and
the native helper and we think they will be prepared
to enter the Theo[logical] Sem[inary] at Samokov in
Sept[ember]. Their progress has been very commendable.

All three young men successfully passed the entrance exam
and were admitted to the American Theological Seminary at
Samokov in September 1878. Gerasim, like so many of his fellow countrymen, was about to embark on a course that would
take him away from Albania. But, unlike the vast majority of
these, he would one day return in service to his people.

Edward Jenney
Special Collections and Archives,
Knox College Library, Galesburg, Illinois.
Used with permission.

CHAPTER 3

SAMOKOV

NOW THE POLITICAL SKIES over European Turkey were dark and threatening. On 24 April 1877, Tsar Alexander II of Russia had declared war on Turkey. The purpose of the Russian campaign was to cross the Balkan Mountains and approach Istanbul as quickly as possible to sever the Slavic states from Ottoman rule and compel the Sultan to make new concessions. To this end Russian and Slavic forces advanced toward Istanbul. The Ottoman lines of defence, often unprepared and in disarray, were repeatedly broken. There was a great battle for the city of Eski Zagra. Here the Turks managed to drive back the Russians for a time and recapture the city, which they razed to the ground and burned. The inhabitants of Eski Zagra were scattered and the mission station was destroyed. The Turks were again repulsed in July 1877. The Russian army moved on.

Concern for the college in Samokov grew daily. In September the missionaries yielded to the 'oft given advice of entreaty' and withdrew to Istanbul. Only one, Edwin Locke, remained behind to do what he could to protect the Mission's property. Jenney joined him on 1 December, after a perilous journey of five days from Monastir. They distributed clothing and supplies to the needy and offered their services at the local hospital, 'binding up the wounds of soldiers'. Their impartial kindness gained them the respect of all sides, Turk, Bulgarian, and Russian.

Then, in the second week of January 1878, it was upon them. The 'siege' began. Locke described those harrowing days.

> When the Turkish troops entered the city they were quartered on the Christians. Fearing that an attempt would be made to occupy our buildings, especially the boarding-school building, I called on the first general in command (Osman Pasha), who received me very cordially. He listened to my request, — that, unless it was really needful, the three houses occupied by us *Americans* might not be occupied by his soldiery, — and referred me to a colonel who had charge of such matters, with a verbal request to him that he would see that our three houses were not taken for the use of the soldiers. The colonel told me to raise our flag, that he might know which our buildings were. We raised it at once, and it has been up to this day.[1]

On 11 January, at one o'clock in the morning, the Turks were in retreat. By daybreak all the army was away, except a few stragglers. At three p.m., 6,500 Russian troops marched into the city. Jenney and Locke stood at the gate of Locke's house, directly under the American flag, and watched them enter, saluting the officers as they passed. Two days later some Cossacks set fire to a barn connected with the mission property but 'thanks to a favoring Providence, it did us no harm'. On Wednesday, 15 January, a detachment of troops arrived, accompanied by a military governor for the city. Five junior officers attempted to force their way into the mission property but the missionaries resisted, insisting that as Americans, they were not obliged to receive them. 'The next day', wrote Locke, 'I called on the officer in command, who received me like a gentleman, returned my call, and has ever shown himself to be very well disposed towards us, not only as Americans, *but as missionaries.*'

Jenney and Locke by their courage and daring had saved the college and mission property, though hours had 'seemed like days, and days weeks'. Samokov and large parts of the Bulgarian territories passed from Turkish to Bulgarian rule. Civilian life gradually returned to its normal pattern. The missionaries decided the school year could continue as planned.

The American Theological College of Samokov first opened on 11 September 1872, with eleven pupils.[2] When Gerasim began there in 1878, the student body numbered eighteen, with eight in his preparatory class. His was one of the last classes to accept students whose expenses were fully covered by the Board.

The college developed considerably during the four years Gerasim studied there. In 1879 permission was granted by the Mission to build a dormitory with a small museum and reading room. This project was completed the following year.

To better define themselves before the new government, the trustees of the school adopted the name, The American Collegiate and Theological Institute. By the time Gerasim graduated in 1882, the student body had grown to over forty.

Gerasim's years at Samokov were instrumental in preparing him for his future task. The opportunity to study subjects such as physics, algebra, geometry, English, and theology under the supervision of well-educated teachers in comfortable surroundings was a rare privilege for someone from European Turkey.

He enjoyed his studies, especially those dealing with science and theology and he excelled in English. To develop their English speaking skills, the students made a rule requiring that only English be spoken during certain hours of the day. Anyone caught conversing in another language during such times had to pay a fine imposed by the students themselves. The money thus raised was devoted to the student library.[3]

One man who made a lasting impression on Gerasim at Samokov was John House, who later founded the prestigious American Farm School in Thessaloniki. House's philosophy of education was to prepare the students spiritually, mentally and practically 'along the things of the heart, the head and the hands, that is the whole man'.[4]

On 27 May 1881, a royal visit caused a flurry of activity and excitement at the school. Prince Alexander von Battenburg, of German descent but related to both the British and Russian royal families, had been named Prince of Bulgaria in April 1879. A brief description of his visit appears in the annual report to the Mission:

> He came, attended by his staff, and after being welcomed by Mr. Clark, made an inspection of the building. He gave voice to much surprise at the provision made for the students in their rooms. The students decorated the building, with enthusiasm, and greeted the Prince with a hymn from our books. In the evening the building was illuminated.[5]

During Gerasim's years at Samokov, political developments further afield served to ignite Albanian passions and catalyse the nationalist movement.

On 31 January 1878, the Russian armies stood poised at the very gates of Istanbul. The British, alarmed at the prospect of Russian domination of the region, had their Mediterranean Fleet anchored in the Dardanelles. Only the threat of war with Britain kept the Russians from taking their prize. Under the circumstances the Ottomans were forced to capitulate and Sultan Abdulhamit II could do little else but accept the stringent terms laid out by the Russians in the Treaty of San Stefano. According to this agreement large portions of the Ottoman Empire were to be conceded to the enemy, including major Albanian-populated territories. The Great Powers, however, disagreed with Russia's demands and called for an international congress to discuss new terms. It opened in Berlin on 13 June 1878 and would eventually set considerable limits on Russian spoils.

Three days earlier on 10 June, over three hundred Albanian delegates from across Albania had gathered at Prizren to form the Albanian League with the purpose of uniting the Albanian peoples and to prevent the secession of Albanian lands to neighbouring nations.[6] Letters were drafted and sent to the foreign ministers of both Turkey and the Great Powers demanding that Albanian territorial integrity be respected. The League also called for the four vilayets of Albania — Monastir, Yanina, Skopje and Shkodra — to be united in a single province. Though some of their demands were heeded and Russian territorial gains reduced, significant portions of ethnically Albanian territory were divided among her neighbours. When in 1880 the Turks also handed over the northern Albanian port of Ulqin to Montenegro, the Albanians responded by attacking Ottoman officials and troops in the area and sabotaging the railroads. The Turkish army brutally suppressed the uprising and crushed the

League, but the struggle for Albanian independence had now well and truly begun.

At the end of the nineteenth century, two forces fiercely opposed the rise of Albanian national consciousness. First, the Ottomans feared that a united Albania would result in irrepressible demands for autonomy, further destabilising the region and weakening Turkey's control over its European foothold. To counter this, the authorities took advantage of the fact that many Albanian families had converted to Islam over the centuries and were now, as Muslims, 'brothers' with the Turks. Schools connected to the mosques taught Turkish and Arabic but the establishment of Albanian language schools, potential nests of sedition, was strongly discouraged. Also, several Albanian Muslims were given high government posts, a fact which, as we shall see, would actually open new doors for the nationalist cause.

Secondly, Greece coveted the territories of southern Albania and vied to secure them when Turkey inevitably lost its grip on Europe. To this end a programme of expansion was developed which involved Hellenising the non-Greek populations of those regions. The Greeks regarded religion as an expression of national identity. Anyone belonging to the Orthodox Church, regardless of ethnicity, was counted as Greek. Greek schools were established and run by the Greek Orthodox Church in the Greek language. In the churches Greek alone was permitted for use in the liturgy and prayers. The priests went so far as to tell the Albanians to pray only in Greek, for God could not understand their language.

Such were the political realities which Gerasim would face and have to overcome. His simple desire to preach and teach in

Albanian would one day thrust him headlong into a dangerous conflict with the most powerful religious and political forces of his day. His years at Samokov proved to be the calm before the storm.

Although he enjoyed his time at school, he never lost his longing for home. Inspiration for the song *Dashuria e Mëmëdheut* [Love of The Land of My Birth], came from this period:

Ah, mëmëdhe i dashur,
që s'munt unë të duroj,
Në dhe të huaj tërë jetën
unë ta shkoj.

Kujtimet s'më lënë të të harroj,
Të mundja fët tani të fluturoj,
Në gji, në gji të nënës sime sot,
Se lumërimin që kam këtu e quaj kot.

Oh, beloved land of my birth,
Can this body endure,
To live beyond your shore?

You rest in my heart, secure.
If I could now but fly,
To my dear mother's side —
What pleases me here is so empty!

The mission records contain little information about Gerasim during these formative years of his life. That Samokov served to shape and mature him is obvious. When he received his diploma in 1882, Gerasim left behind 'an excellent reputation for scholarship, ability, faithfulness, geniality, and piety'.[7]

The stage was now set for what he would call his 'sacred task'. The former shoemaker, trained and ready, would soon dedicate himself in service to his people that they might grow and prosper and reap the benefits that come through the enlightenment of mind and spirit.

Collegiate and Theological Institute at Samokov, Bulgaria.

CHAPTER 4

FIRST TOUR

AFTER GRADUATION GERASIM ATTENDED the 1882 Annual
Meeting of the American Board's Turkish Mission in Istanbul
where it was decided he would oversee a small, Bulgarian-
speaking congregation in Skopje. Now a 'licensed preacher', he
could hold Bible classes, tour, preach, and do other tasks as a
'native worker'. The Mission expected those who, like Gerasim,
had received full scholarships at college to serve for a time with
a minimal salary.

Gerasim, however, had a growing desire to start a work
among his own people. For years missionaries had laboured
among the Greeks, Slavs, and Armenians, establishing mission
stations, churches and schools, but as yet little had been done
for the Albanians.

Gerasim visited his family in Monastir before continuing on
to Skopje. He spoke with the American missionaries about the
possibility of working in Albania. Though enthusiastic, they
could give but little encouragement. Mission funds at that time
were very limited and it was unlikely the Board in America
would consent to opening a new field. John Baird told Gerasim
about Alexander Thomson, a Scottish missionary in Istanbul,

whom he knew to be deeply interested in the Albanian people. Thomson's son, Robert, had recently attended a conference of the mission in Monastir. Upon his return to Istanbul he immediately told his father about Gerasim.

Dr. Alexander Thomson had served as Head Agent for the British and Foreign Bible Society (BFBS) in the Ottoman Empire since 1860. Born in Arbroath, Scotland in 1820, he graduated from Edinburgh University and obtained a professorship in Hebrew in 1843. A gifted linguist, Thomson was fluent in several languages. Ordained by the Free Church of Scotland in 1845, he was sent to Budapest as a missionary to the Jews. Two years later he began a work among the sizable Jewish community in Istanbul and moved with his wife, Eliza, to Bebek, a settlement six miles north of Istanbul on the shores of the Bosphorus.

The aim of the Bible Society was to translate, publish and distribute the Bible or Bible portions in as many languages of the world as possible. Founded in 1804 and supported entirely by voluntary donations, the work of the BFBS soon spanned the globe. In many cases BFBS translations proved instrumental in providing nations not only with the Bible, but with their language for the first time in written form.

The first Albanian New Testament translation, begun in 1819 and printed on Corfu in 1827, was a remarkable achievement considering the limited awareness outside the Balkans at that time of the existence of such a people or language. This translation was revised and reprinted in Athens in 1858.

Thomson visited Albania in 1863 on a trip designed to familiarise him with the Balkans. These first impressions were to remain with him for the rest of his life. Touring Tirana, Berat, and Shkodra, he was overwhelmed by the wanton neglect

and abject poverty he found but, like Lord Byron a generation before, he too was captivated by the Albanians themselves
whom he described as a 'wild but noble race'. From that time he
resolved to do all he could to help them.

Thomson knew that for the work to grow, literature depots
were needed in the country. To this end, in March 1864, a
German named Hermann Riedel was stationed at Shkodra and
in May 1865, Alexander Davidson, a Scot, moved to Yanina to
serve the southern Albanian territories. Under their supervision
colporteurs, or Bible Society booksellers, began to make regular
tours.

While in Shkodra, Thomson observed that the Bible Society's
Albanian version in the southern *Tosk* dialect in Greek letters
was of little use among the northern Albanians who were unfa-
miliar with that alphabet and spoke their own Albanian *Gheg*
dialect. He persuaded the Committee in London to approve his
proposal for a Gheg version using a Latin-based alphabet and
began searching for a competent linguist. In December 1864,
Thomson contacted the Albanian headmaster of a Greek school
in Tunis, a man previously known to the Bible Society. His
name was Konstandin Kristoforidhi. A graduate of St. Julian's
Protestant college in Malta, Kristoforidhi had been introduced
to linguistics as a young man while teaching Gheg to the emi-
nent Austrian albanologist, Johan Georg von Han.

In April 1865, Kristoforidhi agreed to Thomson's terms and
moved, with his family, to Istanbul. Over the next two decades
Kristoforidhi would make a monumental contribution to the
Albanian nation by crystallizing and purifying the Albanian language as he translated the books of the Bible into both Gheg
and Tosk. For this work Kristoforidhi is today regarded as the

'father of the Albanian language' and his statue stands in the centre of his hometown of Elbasan.

Apart from spiritual regeneration, Thomson knew from the history of his own people that education played a fundamental role in securing national prosperity. The Albanians had suffered greatly from its lack. He wrote:

> The Albanian nation has been subjected to a singular and cruel injustice by both its political and ecclesiastical rulers. Though it is an unquestionable axiom that no nation can ever be really educated except through the medium of the vernacular language, the native language was in the case of this people proscribed by the clergy of the Greek Church, who have steadily pursued a Hellenizing policy, and equally neglected by the Turkish and by the Greek governments; for both have numerous subjects who understand no language perfectly but the Albanian.[1]

Unused to reading their own language, few Albanians purchased the Society's translations. To overcome this problem, Kristoforidhi prepared a small Albanian grammar which Thomson was able to publish with private funds in 1882. This little book was to invoke the wrath of both Greek and Turk.

The presence of literature depots and colporteurs distributing Albanian books gradually awakened the interest of the population, but Thomson was keenly aware of the need for a capable Albanian to carry the work forward. Year after year he continued his search for such a man.

And so, when Thomson's son, Robert, returned to Istanbul from the Annual Meeting of the European Turkish Mission in Monastir in July 1882, with news of a promising young Albanian, a graduate of Samokov, Thomson took action. He wrote to the missionaries in Monastir concerning Gerasim, and encouraged them to consider opening an Albanian evening class for the youth of the city:

> We are desirous to attempt something of the sort here, as we have really sold a large number of single gospels to the people. But the Albanians are scattered all over this great city, and it is hard to collect them; and besides we have no man equal to Mr. Kyrias.[2]

Like Thomson, Baird was aware of the unique opportunity afforded by someone of Gerasim's ability and preparation to begin a work among the Albanians. Baird wrote to the Secretary of the American Board in Boston but, as he feared, the Mission was unwilling to sanction a new work at that time. Therefore, when Thomson asked permission to correspond with Gerasim about possible ministry in Albania, the missionaries felt they could not 'protest against a plain providence'.

And so, in a letter written on 27 January 1883, Alexander Thomson presented Gerasim with an astounding invitation written in Greek:

> My Dear Sir,
> I am taking the liberty of writing you a few words, because I know you are Albanian, and therefore long for the gospel of God's grace to reach your countrymen. For many years, since 1863 when I first visited Albania, and read the history of the nation, and how Skanderbeg (George Castriotis) fought for his nation, I have been very concerned for the people, and have sought to distribute

among them the word of God, as the best means of stirring up the people to spiritual life. Among the Tosks there was a little interest, but no books, or very few, were sold to the Ghegs. I believe the translations of the New Testament and Psalter are good, but since I do not know the Albanian language, I would very much like to know what you think about them, that is, of the Gheg and Tosk translations. When I think about the Albanians it seems to me that the great necessity is for us to have schools where the children can learn their own language, with the word of God, and where we can preach to them the Saviour Jesus, the friend of sinners. And not only in Albania, but also here in Constantinople, where we have many Albanians. Unfortunately the translator K. Kristoforidhi is not an active Christian, and cannot, or will not, preach to his countrymen. I would very much like to know what you think about the work for them, and if you would not wish, nay, long to be the evangelist of your nation. Please write me what you think we should do, or seek to do.

Before ever receiving it, Gerasim had already written to Thomson in English. Their letters crossed paths. Gerasim explained he had considered writing earlier, but had not dared to do so. Though he knew from Baird of Thomson's interest in Albania, it was not until he arrived in Skopje and heard the same from Seefried, the Bible Society's colporteur there, that he 'took courage and began to inquire into the matter'. He was moved by what he had heard of Thomson's 'great desire to have the gospel preached to the Albanians', and prayed he would 'achieve the end he sought in the spiritual regeneration of the nation'. To better understand the needs of the country, Gerasim proposed 'to visit with a

companion the principal cities and large villages of Albania —
taking the necessary books'.³ Would Thomson approve?

Thomson, who for so many years had sought after an Albanian to labour among his own people, saw in Gerasim God's
providential provision. In turn, Gerasim recognised in Thomson
the potential to realise his dream of working in Albania.

Before any formal association could be established, the
problem of Gerasim's relationship with the American Mission,
which had trained and prepared him at their expense, had to be
resolved. Thomson explained his intentions to the Americans in
a letter written on 2 February 1883.⁴

Though the missionaries were reluctant to part with
Gerasim, who gave 'promise of great usefulness', they allowed
him to choose as he deemed best. Without hesitation Gerasim
chose the Bible Society and Albania. It would doubtless prove
to be the hardest path.

The challenges facing the work of the Bible Society in the
Ottoman Empire were considerable. Despite various charters
and treaties guaranteeing basic human rights and freedoms, and
the provisions protecting the Bible Society's activity which bore
the signature of the Sultan himself, in practice many Turkish
authorities strongly opposed them. Thomson was well aware
of the difficulties. 'The government seems resolved to annoy
both us and the Americans by every sort of impediment to missionary work and especially to colportage in Albania'.⁵ Old laws
were amended and new laws introduced with surprising regularity, making the process of translating, printing and distributing literature long and tedious.

Before publication, all books had to be sanctioned by the
Imperial Censor and carry his seal of approval on the title page.

A further stamp was required from the local authorities before they could be sold. Also, colporteurs had to carry special permits not required of other traders. To obtain all the necessary seals and permissions, weeks and even months could be lost in a labyrinth of bureaucracy.

Nor was it uncommon for the colporteurs to meet with physical abuse, especially in the Albanian provinces following the establishment of the League of Prizren. One of Thomson's men, Clement Sovnoski, was murdered as he left Prizren in 1879. Thomson's present colporteurs for the Albanian territories, Sevastides and Seefried, suffered frequent beatings and expulsions. The Turks would oppose anyone who threatened to stir up or agitate the local population.

But there were also weaknesses in Ottoman administration, particularly in the outlying provinces. When, for example, the authorities banned the sale of the Society's Tosk Albanian books in April 1883, Thomson expressed little concern. His experience in Turkey had shown that 'often the orders of the government become useless in a very short space of time'.[6]

Gerasim now awaited the approval of the BFBS Committee in London for his trip. Meanwhile Thomson tried, unsuccessfully, to get him a sales permit, but Gerasim was willing to attempt the tour with his Ottoman passport alone.

While they waited, Gerasim told Thomson of his desire to study medicine in America or England for he saw a 'great work before him', and wished to prepare for it as soon as possible.[7] Thomson sought support for this from friends, but none responded.

Then, on 3 May 1883, Gerasim received the telegram from Thomson that changed the course of the rest of his life:

BEGIN THE JOURNEY. SOCIETY ENGAGES YOU.

Gerasim could scarcely contain his excitement. He told Thomson he was going 'with great joy and hope on this tour', and 'prayed for the Spirit of power'.[8] The next day he left for Monastir. Seefried followed a few days later.

Thomson reminded him of the purpose of the tour, that they were 'not to go too quickly from place to place, but to try and speak with all classes of the people in each place, and offer them the word of God. I am also very desirous that you should speak to the Albanians in their own language, and read the gospels to them, that they may be convinced that these holy things can be expressed in Albanian'.[9] Gerasim stayed with his family for a few days before setting off with Seefried.

They arrived in Kortcha on 14 May 1883. It was Gerasim's first visit to Albania and he was very encouraged by what he found. 'The Albanians', he wrote, 'are nobler and less fanatical than the other nations in Turkey'.[10] His public readings of the Albanian scriptures aroused much interest and curiosity. They sold many Albanian New Testaments, as well as Gheg and Tosk Old Testament Histories, Kristoforidhi's Tosk grammar, the Tosk children's catechisms and other books.

Leaving Kortcha at the end of May, they travelled through Permet to Berat where they met Sevastides on 1 June. Seefried returned to Skopje and Gerasim continued his tour with Sevastides. They left for Kavaya two weeks later.

When they arrived in Kavaya they were immediately summoned to court by the local kaymakam who closely examined their passports and documents before allowing them to return to their *khan*, or inn. The next day as they went out to sell they were confronted by a *zaptieh*, or policeman, and ordered to return to the court. This time their books were examined and those not bearing the stamp of the district censor's office were collected into two boxes and held. Also, a letter was written to the pasha of Durres explaining the situation.

On Saturday, at Gerasim's request, the kaymakam allowed them to continue selling their stamped books, but early Monday morning a telegram arrived from the pasha of Durres demanding that Gerasim and Sevastides be sent there.

They soon realised they had been under observation since leaving Kortcha. In Permet the authorities had refused to stamp their passports, but they continued regardless. The authorities in Berat questioned them for not having had their passports stamped in Permet. They would have been turned back but for Thomson who, in response to an earlier plea from Sevastides over a different matter, had contacted the British Embassy. When a telegram arrived from Istanbul authorizing Sevastides to sell his books, the Berat officials, unaware it had no bearing on the present situation, released them both. But now the authorities were determined to stop them.

Gerasim protested strongly to the kaymakam of Kavaya against their unjust treatment. He reminded the official that both he and Sevastides were Ottoman citizens. Their passports were in order. Most of the books were stamped, and all bore the seal of the Censorship in Istanbul. Gerasim's appeals fell on deaf ears.

Six zaptiehs held them in the market until they were taken under guard to Durres and handed over to the jailer. Two hours later the mutasarrif of Durres was notified of their arrival. He called for them and demanded they either produce a *kefil*, a person to stand as bail or guarantor, or be thrown back into prison.

Gerasim again appealed against the injustice of such actions. This time he found sympathy with the mutasarrif, who took them to see the pasha.

The pasha demanded to know: 'What are you?'

'We are booksellers,' they said.

The pasha asked: 'Are you Protestants?'

'Yes,' they replied.

He continued: 'Have you no permit for the books you sell?'

Gerasim said: 'No, but our passports are in order and our books are sacred Scriptures printed in Constantinople with the permission of the Censor.'

The pasha demanded they either produce a kefil or remain in jail. Gerasim explained they were Ottoman citizens employed by a foreign company, their papers were in order and they were strangers in Durres. Under such circumstances, he asked, could not the pasha himself stand as kefil? Impressed by his boldness, the pasha agreed publicly with the request, but Gerasim later overheard him tell the mutasarrif not to release them until they provided a kefil.

They were then taken back to the prison courtyard and again told if they were to avoid further imprisonment, someone must stand bail for them. Eventually they sent for Lazarus Theocharides, a clerk with Gregorio Lauda of Berat who owned a depot in Durres that was used by the Bible Society. Theocharides arrived and agreed to stand as kefil. As soon as they were released, Gerasim went to the mutasarrif to ask permission to sell their stamped books, but this time his request was denied. The pasha had yet to decide their fate.

Gerasim went straight to the telegraph office and sent the following message to Thomson:

FROM KAVAYA WERE SENT TO PRISON IN DURRES
— WE ARE UNDER KEFIL.

Thomson was away from the office and did not receive the telegram until two days later when he immediately informed the
British Embassy of the arrest.[11] The British chargé d'affaires,
Hugh Wyndham, directed his staff 'to inquire thoroughly into
the causes of this proceeding'.[12]

The embassy acted 'promptly and energetically', informing the Sublime Porte that the British government strongly
objected to the wrongful arrest of employees of British agencies. The Porte sent orders to the pasha of Durres to release the
booksellers and allow them to resume their work.

Meanwhile in Durres Gerasim and Sevastides sat waiting. On
Thursday, 21 June, a zaptieh arrived and said: 'The pasha wants
you.'

They went at once, greeting the pasha as they entered his
office. Without returning their salutation he shouted: 'Take
your books hence! Who imprisoned you as you telegraphed to
Constantinople?'

Gerasim reminded the pasha of their treatment at the hands of
the kaymakam and mutasarrif, their detention in Kavaya, the trip
to Durres under guard, their confinement in jail and the terms of
the kefil. These were the reasons they had sent the telegram. But
with the situation now resolved, Gerasim continued, would not
the pasha give them a letter 'to prevent their suffering in the same
way at Tirana?' The pasha refused and threw them out.

They continued to Vlora, Elbasan and Tirana, returning
to Durres on 26 June. Gerasim intended to visit Shkodra, but
Sevastides, having recently been expelled from that city, had had

enough and would accompany him no further. Gerasim sent
a telegram to Kirby Green, the British consul in Shkodra, to
ask if the Ottoman authorities would permit his coming. Green
responded on 28 June that he would not be interfered with. And
so, as Gerasim made his way to Shkodra alone, his first tour of
Albania neared its end.

The former shoemaker's apprentice had shown he could
handle himself well in the face of adversity, but he was discon-
certed by the deliberate obstruction of the authorities. How
were they to work when they met with constant opposition?
What could be accomplished if most of their time was spent
in the courts? In the seven days from leaving Berat, they had
'wrought only one day free'.[13]

For Thomson, however, the tour represented a resounding
triumph. The British Embassy had come to their defence and the
Turkish authorities had backed down. But most important of
all, Gerasim had been received with enthusiasm by the people.

Though previously supportive of his plans to study abroad,
Thomson was now convinced that a time had come when
much could be won for Albania. Did Gerasim really need further schooling when he was already educated far above the rest
of his nation? His knowledge of Greek and English gave him
access to a wide variety of books and literature, which he could
study on his own. Would he not stay for the sake of his people?
'We must fight out the battle', wrote Thomson, 'whatever pains
and trouble it may cost us'.[14]

> But in truth, it seems to me, my dear Sir, that if you wish
> to evangelize your own nation, you already have all the
> education you require. What they need is the gospel

preached to them in their own language, and this, by God's grace, you are able as an Agent of this Society to give them. Is this not the call of God to you? Think and pray over this, and tell me your thoughts.[15]

Gerasim was to travel to Istanbul at the end of July. There they would discuss how best to proceed with the work, where he should live, the choice of colporteurs, and more. But when he returned to Monastir, he was stricken by 'some illness in his face probably produced by his tour', delaying his trip to the capital. Writing from Istanbul in August 1883, Thomson made a final appeal:

> I think when we meet you will agree that this is a time when much may be won, or much may be lost for the cause of God and of civilization among your people, and I am sure you are too much of a patriot to desert their cause at this critical moment.[16]

With this challenge in mind, Gerasim arrived in Istanbul at the beginning of September. The outcome of the next few months would prove crucial in determining his future role in Albania.

Alexander Thomson
From the BFBS archives at Cambridge University Library
Used with permission

Young Gerasim Kyrias, ca. 1878
Courtesy of Hristo and Oliver Kirjas,
used with permission.

CHAPTER 5

ISTANBUL

NOW THE TURKISH AUTHORITIES faced an unexpected challenge. As a result of their aggressive policies toward the Albanian national movement and all its causes, the Albanian League had been crushed, its leaders imprisoned or sent into exile. The Albanian provinces were under a virtual state of military rule with the local authorities on the alert against the slightest hint of any 'subversive' activity. But it seemed the movement had been embraced by an unexpected champion. The British and Foreign Bible Society, with the apparent support of the British government, demanded the right to publish and distribute Albanian books. This was a problem the Turkish authorities had not anticipated. How could they curb the activities of an agency whose interests were protected by one of the Great Powers?

For years the BFBS had printed and distributed small quantities of Albanian scriptures with limited opposition. But the publication of Kristoforidhi's grammar in 1882, while the League of Prizren still troubled Turkish minds, brought a sharp change in government policy. Distribution of the grammar with other Albanian books might lead to the widespread use of Albanian as a written language. Such potential to unify the Albanians posed a serious threat to Turkish interests. This objection, however, could not be stated openly. Other reasons would be found to thwart the work of the Bible Society.

The Sublime Porte accused Gerasim and Sevastides of having lied about their detention in Durres. The kaymakam, the mutasarrif, and the pasha all denied any wrongdoing. They claimed the men had not been arrested, nor even threatened with arrest. Their books had been examined, nothing more. If there had been a delay it was only because some of their books had not been properly stamped.

The Porte demanded an explanation from Wyndham who contacted the Bible Society. Thomson resolutely defended the testimony of his men.

Two major obstacles now confronted the Bible Society's future work in Albania. First, the government refused to sanction further publication of Tosk scriptures in the Greek alphabet. Second, the authorities were preventing shipments of Albanian scriptures from reaching Albania. For several months four cases of books intended for Yanina were held in the customs house at Prevesa in southern Albania. By thus refusing to allow the publication of new materials while keeping existing supplies from reaching the depots, the Turks could effectively subvert the Society's activities.

At the end of September, Hugh Wyndham was replaced by a full ambassador, the former governor general of Canada, Frederick Hamilton-Temple-Blackwood, the Earl of Dufferin. It is interesting to note that at his first meeting with the Turkish government, the new ambassador, among other matters of state, received an official explanation of Ottoman policy regarding the Bible Society and Albania.

On 6 October 1883, Thomson received a letter from the British Embassy informing him the Turkish authorities did not approve of the use of the Greek alphabet for any Albanian dialect 'on political grounds.' Furthermore, due to the 'unsettled state of Albania,' it was unlikely they would allow the continued free circulation of Albanian scriptures.

Thomson was incensed. In a lengthy rebuttal he dismissed the Sublime Porte's arguments as fatuous. The Bible Society had long used its Greek-based alphabet among the southern Albanians without the slightest provocation. Furthermore, he challenged inquiry into 'whether the circulation of the Word of God in Albanian, Greek, Turkish, and other languages by [BFBS] agents, has ever led to the least disturbance of the peace, or to the slightest disaffection of the people.' Thomson accused the government itself of using 'groundless violence' against the colporteurs and concluded his letter with an appeal to the ambassador:

As it is impossible for me to accept the reasons assigned by the Ottoman authorities as a sufficient justification of their procedure, I can only remit the matter to your Excellency, and beg that every opportunity may be embraced of procuring from the government liberty to circulate the Word of God freely in Albania in the only language which the mass of the population can understand, though as yet but few can read it.[1]

Thomson spoke at length with Gerasim concerning these matters, who had begun to familiarise himself with both the Bible Society and the city of Istanbul. It was a promising field.

Indeed we have found that this capital is a most important station for operating on the whole Albanian people, in consequence of its being the centre to which thousands come every year from Albania, that they may resort to the various provinces round about for employment, especially during the summer months.[2]

Economic stagnation in Albania, with widespread poverty and unemployment, had led many Albanians to seek work in major cities such as Bucharest, Sofia, Alexandria, and Istanbul. In the evenings these men would gather in the coffee houses and inns which often bore the names of their home towns and villages, to pass the time discussing the politics of the day, and to share their concerns and bits of news and other information. It was here, in such environments, that new patriotic societies were born.

One family at the centre of the nationalist movement in Istanbul were the Frasheris from Permet in southern Albania. Three brothers, Abdyl, Naim and Sami, laboured tirelessly for the Albanian cause.

A former member of the Turkish Parliament, Abdyl, became leader of the League of Prizren in 1878, eventually heading the delegation sent by the League to defend Albanian territorial integrity before the governments of Europe. For this action he was condemned to death, the Sultan eventually commuting his sentence to life imprisonment. After serving three years of his sentence, he was released in 1884, due to poor health and probably the intervention of his now influential younger brother, Naim.

Naim had risen from serving as a lowly customs officer in Saranda in southern Albania to a high post in the Censor's office under the Ministry of Education in 1882. He has been called 'the spirit of Albania' for his inspirational poetic writings such as 'Albania,' and the epic 'History of Skanderbeg.' His numerous works stirred the patriotic sentiments of the Albanians and spurred large numbers from indifference into action.

Sami, the youngest of the three, was a gifted linguist and author and a driving force behind the development of a single Albanian alphabet for the whole nation, a dream which, unfortunately, was not fulfilled in his lifetime. Like Kristoforidhi, he too published a grammar that was printed in 1879 using his 'Istanbul Alphabet.' That same year he formed a committee in Istanbul called the 'Society for Publication of Albanian Literature,' which aimed to oversee both literature preparation and the establishment of Albanian schools.

It was into this circle of visionaries and activists that Gerasim now entered, aged twenty-five, already burning with a vision of his own for his beloved Albania.

Through Kristoforidhi Gerasim would have met these and other influential Albanians in the capital, discussing Albania's needs. He met too with his fellow countrymen, 'urging upon them the claims of the great Salvation, and pointing out the necessity of using the national language in order to convey sacred truth, and indeed all education whatever to all classes and both sexes of the people.'[3] He was alarmed, however, to find that colporteurs were scorned, a fact which severely impaired his ability to share his message, for few cared to listen to the words of a 'mere book-seller.' Much to Thomson's dismay, Gerasim developed an aversion to such work. Nor had he understood that the BFBS was a Bible *selling* society, but had thought, as with the American Mission, he could be employed simply to preach the gospel. This was not the case and though Gerasim was willing to oversee, direct and encourage colportage, he could not, or would not sell. In view of this, Thomson sent letters to various mission agencies seeking financial support for Gerasim to start a mission work among his own people.

In the evenings the young preacher studied Gheg with Kristoforidhi. He also began preparing a new Tosk primer and religious tracts and materials for publication. In the early months of 1884 he wrote the first Albanian language hymns:

O sa i bukurë mëngjes!
Gjith' bota po thërret;
I ëmbël zë dëgjoetë
Iisuj u ngjall vërtet!
O besëtarët e Iisujt,
Mos qani për atë
Shikoni këtë var të Ti,
Qysh mbet i xbrazëtë,
Andaj mos qani Krishti ron
Dhe lum ay që i beson!

O glorious day!
The whole world 'round;
Echoes the sound:
Jesus is risen indeed!
O you who believe,
Hush, do not grieve! —
The grave where he lay,
Stands empty today,
So weep no more, but be ever sure:
Blessed are those who believe!

His hymns were sung at special Albanian worship services held each Sunday. He was assisted in these meetings by John Tsiku, a newly acquired Albanian colporteur from Kortcha.

Gerasim had now given up his plans to study abroad and felt one of the most pressing needs was to establish a day school 'in which the youngest might be taught to read the Scriptures and other books ... in Albanian.'[4] This idea was the seed from which one day would spring a full-time school for girls, eventually involving both his sisters and dozens of others. But for now the problem of his support remained unresolved.

He had agreed initially to a three-month contract with the Bible Society while they sought a more permanent arrangement. In February his contract was extended for an additional three months, but during that time it was imperative they find a satisfactory solution.

In March, an old friend and former classmate of Thomson's, Thomas Brown, then Secretary of the Turkish Missions Aid Society, wrote to inform them his mission had agreed to give Gerasim £25 a year on a two-year trial basis. This was an encouragement, but £25 was not enough. No other mission responded.

Under these circumstances Thomson made an unusual proposal to his Committee. If they would agree to pay £25 a year for Gerasim to superintend the colporteurs and oversee a depot, the grant from the Turkish Missions Aid Society could go toward his preaching and missionary activities. Thomson suggested Kortcha for Gerasim's place of residence and recommended they hire four colporteurs, two for Yanina and the south, and two for northern and central Albania.

When Gerasim heard of the proposal he told Thomson he could not manage on £50 per year. He had accepted a minimal wage in Skopje because of his debt to the American mission, but to live in Albania would require at least £72 a year plus house rent. Thomson informed the Committee, adding that he considered it a reasonable request.

Then came the challenge of hiring suitable colporteurs. Thomson knew such men were 'as hard to find as nuggets of gold, and good ones are as precious as such nuggets'. Tsiku had proven himself a reliable worker and Gerasim suggested two others, one of whom was Jovancho, a Bulgarian watchmaker from Prishtina, and member of the Protestant church there.

But their problems with the Turkish government remained unresolved. As long as the Bible Society could neither print nor distribute Albanian literature, the Committee in London would not employ Gerasim for that field.

And then, suddenly and unexpectedly, a light dawned. At the end of March, permission arrived from the Ministry of Education to print the Tosk scriptures. Thomson attributed this breakthrough to Gerasim's intervention and his association with Naim Frasheri and the Albanian Committee of Istanbul. Final preparation of the text began immediately. However, the problem of distributing Albanian literature in the Albanian provinces remained unresolved.

On 1 April 1884, Thomson received a letter from the British ambassador informing him that considerable correspondence had taken place between the Grand Vizier, Küçük Sait Pasha, and the Ministry of Education concerning the Bible Society's books held at Prevesa. Sait Pasha was the Sultan's chief instrument in the cabinet, responsible to develop a programme for restoring centralised control of the provinces.[5] Opposing Albanian books 'on political grounds,' Sait Pasha had himself given the order to detain the cases at Prevesa.[6] Here at last was proof that resistance to the Society's work came from the highest levels. The ambassador requested a meeting with Thomson who wrote his Committee:

> You can easily suppose that the proceedings of the Grand Vizier have caused us no small perplexity as to how to prosecute our Albanian work, apart altogether from the question of the engagement of Mr. Kyrias. The treaty of Berlin distinctly indicated that Albania was to be treated more as a unity than formerly, but that, I suspect, the Porte won't do it unless under compulsion; for it is anxious to retain its hold on that province as long as possible in its fragmentary form, under which it can give the preponderating influence to the Moslems.[7]

With these difficulties in mind, Gerasim put forward a new plan. Rather than establish a base in Kortcha where they would attract unwelcome attention, he suggested settling in Monastir, 'where there are American missionaries, and where his own father and his family reside.' With more than one thousand Albanian families in that town, he would have ample opportunity to meet with Albanians and, being near to Albania proper, he could also find ways to take Scriptures there. Thomson agreed, but the Committee remained undecided.

Then, as suddenly and unexpectedly as the first, the second obstacle disappeared. Months after the books were detained at Prevesa, supplies in Yanina had dwindled to nothing. The Bible Society Superintendent there, Stavros Michaelides, asked Thomson to send Greek and Turkish scriptures without any Albanian books. When two cases of Greek and Hebrew scriptures arrived at Prevesa in March, the mutasarrif refused to allow them through, asserting he had orders to hold all shipments of books until further notice. Thomson then had two cases of Turkish books 'specially sealed so that they ought not to be opened till they arrived at their destination in Yanina.' He also contacted the British consul in Prevesa and asked him 'to urge the observance of the rule in this case.' When the Turkish scriptures arrived at the customs house in Prevesa the mutasarrif, apparently tired of the troublesome affair, had all the cases collected and sent off to the vali of Yanina, effectively handing responsibility over to his superior.[8]

Meanwhile the vali of Yanina, at the request of Michaelides months earlier, had already examined samples of the Albanian books in question and declared them harmless. Possibly in ignorance of the Grand Vizier's orders, or for reasons known only to himself, when the cases arrived in Yanina, the vali passed them directly to the Bible Society superintendent.

With both problems resolved, the BFBS Committee in London agreed to sanction Gerasim's employment. Their decision arrived in Istanbul on 19 April 1884. That same day Gerasim signed a contract accepting his appointment with the Bible Society as 'Depositary and Superintendent of Colportage at Monastir,' but not, as some have contended, replacing Kristoforidhi in his role as translator with the Bible Society. Gerasim's duties were to include directing the colporteur (Tsiku at that point), keeping his accounts and sending regular reports to Istanbul. He was also to make tours as often as necessary and take every opportunity to press on the people of all nationalities 'that in the present condition of affairs, when no instruction as to the will of God is given in the church, it is the duty of everyone who seeks to serve God to possess and study carefully the written Word.' All this he undertook 'in dependence on divine strength faithfully to perform.'

Gerasim began to prepare for his departure. Books were selected and packed in cases, but as they were about to set off on 12 May, Thomson fell dangerously ill. Two weeks later he struggled to give final instructions to Gerasim and Tsiku and sent them on their way.

The pair travelled by train to Thessaloniki where they met Peter Crosbie, a gifted Scottish missionary and friend of Thomson's who had considerable influence with the Turkish authorities. Crosbie took Gerasim with his cases of books to the censor of the Vilayet of Macedonia. With the memory of his first tour still fresh in his mind, Gerasim was determined to have each volume stamped to guarantee their free circulation throughout the province. The censor assured him, however, that a more liberal policy was now taken regarding the 'sacred books of the Jews and Christians.' It was sufficient, he claimed, for just one sample of each book to bear the required stamp. Despite his misgivings Gerasim had to concede.

Crosbie also introduced Gerasim to the British consul-general at Thessaloniki, J. Elijah Blunt. Blunt kindly provided him with a letter of recommendation for the Austrian consul at Monastir who at that time also served as vice-consul for British interests.

On Sunday, 8 June, Gerasim held an Albanian worship service at the Protestant church of Thessaloniki and was very surprised when ten people came — they had never attained to such a number in Istanbul.

Gerasim arrived in Monastir on 10 June, where he was warmly received by his family and the American missionaries.

With some apprehension, he took his books to the local authorities who, to his astonishment, stamped them all 'without any hesitation.'

He found a house to rent for the depot and arranged a public reading there. On Sunday, 22 June 1884, they held their first Albanian worship service in Monastir. Thirty-six Albanians attended.

Wherever he went he was well received and many expressed a desire to learn to read Albanian. Tsiku soon sold a good number of Albanian volumes. Both men felt a sense of excitement in their new work and Gerasim was very encouraged by what he perceived as an 'extremely favourable beginning.' Little did he know the greatest trial of his life was now before him.

Bible House, Istanbul
Built in 1872.

CHAPTER 6

CAPTURED BY BRIGANDS

THE ARRIVAL IN MONASTIR of a young, educated, well-spoken and energetic Albanian in the service of the British and Foreign Bible Society soon came to the attention of both the secular and religious authorities. The foreign missionaries, protected to varying degrees by foreign powers, had to be tolerated, but an Ottoman subject who openly proclaimed Protestant faith in the Albanian language was looking for trouble. Attempts were soon underway to hinder him, though Gerasim successfully 'defended his liberty to preach and to sell against the intrigues of the Greek Bishop and of the Turkish Governor, who was but too ready to lend himself to injustice'.[1]

There was much to do. They moved the supplies from the depot in Berat to Monastir and Gerasim ordered more books from Istanbul for Tsiku to make an extended tour of the Albanian territories. Thomson reminded him of the importance of keeping careful records. It was on the basis of Tsiku's sales that the Committee in London would decide their request for additional colporteurs. Gerasim managed the public reading room where he received visitors daily. He also continued his linguistic studies and prepared various texts and materials.

In a report written in Monastir on 21 August 1884, a Uniate priest noted meeting a young Albanian Protestant 'who was engaged in special studies of his own language to which he had given himself body and soul and who was attempting to publish a very original grammar'.[2]

Thomson also visited Gerasim at the end of October. Having spent a month at special mineral baths in Switzerland to restore his health, Thomson stopped off in Monastir on his return to Istanbul. He was 'delighted to find Mr. Kyrias vigorously at work, cheerful and hopeful, and highly esteemed by the missionaries of the Board to whom he had long been known as a distinguished student of theology'.[3]

Long hours were spent discussing the work. Seefried was struggling in Skopje, for the vali of Kosova strongly resisted him. Also, Seefried's family suffered frequent illness so it was decided to bring him to Monastir, a healthier city than Skopje, where he could work under Gerasim's direct supervision. Jovancho, the watchmaker from Prishtina, replaced Seefried in Skopje. With the arrival in Kosova of a new vali, Faik Pasha, they hoped the employment of a colporteur native to the region might open the way for the Society's labours.

They also spoke at length about George, Gerasim's nineteen-year-old brother. A member of the Protestant church, George planned to begin his studies at the Theological Institute in Samokov that autumn. Thomson pledged ten Turkish lira a year from his own pocket toward George's education on condition that upon graduation 'he give himself to Albanian work'.

Thomson also attended Gerasim's Albanian worship service. His report of this event was published in the Turkish Missions Aid Society's periodical, *The Star in the East*, in January 1885:

His Albanian service was held at 9 a.m. on the Lord's day. The room was quite filled with a most attentive audience of thirty-six persons, including three women and four children. After an opening prayer a hymn was sung, Mr. Kyrias having written on one side of a black-board three verses of a hymn to be sung at the beginning of the service, and on the other side three verses of another to be sung at the close, the hymns being of his own composition. Another prayer and the reading of the Scriptures followed, and then came the sermon. I presume I am not mistaken in supposing that these services are the first that have presented the simple Gospel to the Albanian people for at least a thousand years...[4]

In an interesting diversion, Skender Luarasi recounted the following story, all the more surprising considering that, on the whole, he avoided the religious aspects of his subject matter:

The children of the neighborhood would often approach him. Gerasim would close his book, embrace them and begin talking with them about things close to their hearts.

'He speaks like Christ!', said one of the little ones. Many of these who came from Albanian homes, where Albanian was spoken, went on Sundays to the Protestant mission hall, when they learned that Gerasim Kyrias was to preach, so they could hear him speak like Christ.

'He is like Christ!', said others; and soon they all began to say, 'He is Christ!'

Luarasi explained that these were harmless words spoken by 'children and simple people'. 'However,' he continued, 'the words Albanian, Protestant, and that an Albanian was called

"Christ" struck like arrows into the heart of Bishop Kristomos, and everyone else in Monastir'.[5]

Gerasim approached his responsibilities with a passion that grew out of his faith and strong sense of calling. He also had a profound impact on his family, especially his sister, Sevasti, who was then twelve years old. She recalled her brother's influence at this time:

> He was happy to hear of the good work I was doing at school and took special care to impress upon me the true value of education and the necessity of working for the enlightenment and uplift of our people. It was he who taught me to read and write my mother tongue. The spirit of patriotism which he sewed in my heart thrust its roots deep and bore fruit in later years.[6]

Sevasti loved the reading room. In her memoirs she recalls looking in awe upon the vast number of books on the shelves and how Gerasim took special care to show her the Albanian volumes. She would bring her friends along so they could see that Albanians too had books in their own language.

One day Gerasim toured the neighbouring town of Krushevo where he preached in Albanian, selling off all the scriptures he had taken. He then planned to revisit Kortcha, a city which had greatly impressed him on his tour in 1883, and where Tsiku had recently sold well. He arranged a carriage and prepared for the journey.

Somewhere, someone was watching and planning his demise. Though never able to make a direct link, as events unfolded long shadows of doubt fell ominously at the door of the Greek Orthodox Bishop.

Unaware of his danger, Gerasim started for Kortcha on 12 November 1884, in the company of a Greek woman whose daughter taught at a school there. The autumn sky was clear and bright and Gerasim was in high spirits. As the carriage passed Lake Prespa, he likened it to 'a mass of molten glass among the mountains'. Waterfowl hunted fish in the distance.

In his book, *Captured By Brigands*, translated by John Baird and published in English in London in 1902, Gerasim recalls hoping to find a suitable place for preaching in Kortcha. 'I was rejoicing in the thought that I was going on such a blessed errand,' he wrote. Luarasi contended in his biography that Gerasim only occasionally accepted to preach in Albanian because of his work with the Bible Society. 'Not to propagate the word of God,' he wrote, 'but to speak to the Albanians in their mother tongue to awaken their love for it and for the Albanian cause'.[7] Luarasi was unaware that the sole aim of the Bible Society was for the production and sales of Bible literature, an aim that did not include preaching. It was precisely Gerasim's desire to preach in Albanian that nearly prevented his employment in the first place. Any preaching he did was entirely at his own initiative.

In the evening they arrived at the village of Stenya where they spent the night in a miserable one-room khan. An open fire blazed in the centre of the room and zaptiehs and muleteers sat on rush mats drinking *raki* and singing loudly while the innkeeper scolded his servants for not doing their work. The smoke and noise continued through the night, keeping the weary travellers from their sleep.

Long before sunrise they paid the innkeeper and resumed their journey. Relieved to be on the road again, Gerasim told the driver: 'I have escaped from that khan.'

After travelling in darkness for two hours they arrived at a guardhouse and rested briefly. Gerasim gave both guards a small gift and they set off again. Suddenly, the driver slowed his horses. Gerasim urged him to speed up but he refused, saying: 'It is a stony place.'

As they approached a blind ravine near Laithiza, they suddenly heard the sound of voices in the woods and saw branches moving near the road. What followed was a sight Gerasim would never forget.

Six or seven 'wild mountaineers with awful faces, rough-speaking and low-minded creatures', armed with rifles, knives and pistols, descended single-file into the gully in front of them. Their heads were tied up with black cloths and their beards were matted. Their *fustanellas*, or white plaited kilts, were blackened and filthy. Each of them wore a *gunga*, or thick sheepskin coat, and under these some bore silver ornaments. They stopped the carriage and ordered Gerasim to get out. As he stepped down they asked: 'Where is your money?'

Gerasim heard a noise behind him and turned to see several other brigands approaching. Among them was their leader, Shahin Matraku, whom they called 'Captain.' He spoke harshly to Gerasim to frighten him into silence.

Shahin was a notorious outlaw from the small, stone village of Popchishta, high in the mountains northwest of Kortcha. He first came into conflict with the authorities as a young man when, after the death of his father, much of his family's property was confiscated for debt. Left without means to support himself, Shahin turned to extortion and soon made many enemies. Together with his brother, he fled into the mountains.

Eventually they were captured and taken to the jail in Kortcha. One night they attempted to escape, but were discovered in the prison yard. The guards opened fire on them, wounding Shahin in the shoulder and killing his brother. Shahin spent the next five years languishing in Monastir prison, where he 'learned better his wicked trade, and resolved to resume it'. Released in 1876, he returned home, gathered a band of men and took to the mountains. His infamy soon spread and he was greatly feared. His many exploits earned him a reputation for ruthlessness and cunning.

Shahin's men worked nervously to empty the carriage and rob the occupants of their valuables. They carefully searched Gerasim's clothes for money but found none. When food and bread were discovered, they 'dropped all other things and fell to devouring it'.

Suddenly a voice rang out from the heights: 'In the Zvezda Pass about twenty cavalrymen have appeared and they are riding rapidly!'

Shahin shouted at his men to hurry and ordered two of them to take Gerasim up the mountain. They ran behind him, forcing him on. One struck him hard in the side with the butt of his rifle and snarled: 'Hurry or I'll kill you!' Others made the driver carry a bag of plunder and follow after.

When the Turkish soldiers arrived at the carriage, the distraught Greek woman told them what had happened. They immediately began firing upon the brigands in flight, showering bullets over their heads. One whistled past Gerasim's ear. As he ran, he began to fear for his life. His thoughts turned to his family.

The brigands gathered to rest at the top of a mountain pass near a spring of cool water. There were twenty-two of them.

Shahin approached Gerasim and pulled a pen from his belt and a sheet of paper from his breast and thrust them at him, demanding: 'Write, 'Send us here five hundred liras,' and say to them that if in ten days the money is not sent us, we will send them your head.'

Gerasim refused, saying: 'I have no money.'

At this, one of the brigands loaded a cartridge into his rifle and said: 'We kill those who have no money to give us.'

Gerasim again refused, insisting it was better for them to kill him there and then than that both they and he should suffer for nothing.

Shahin flew into a rage and shouted: 'You write what we tell you. As for the money, that is our business.'

Unable to do otherwise, Gerasim wrote the following words:

Dear Parents,
    I have been captured by brigands, and they want five hundred liras ransom.
    Gerasim D. Kyrias
    Dry Mountain, November 13, 1884

Handing back the note, Gerasim insisted: 'I tell you now that I have no money, and that there is no place where it can be found. You will labor in vain, and will cause my destruction. My parents are poor, and it is only two years since I left school.' No one believed him.

They gave the note to the driver and told him to take it to Gerasim's family in Monastir. As Gerasim watched him run through the brush and down the mountain he thought to himself wistfully: 'How fortunate you are. I am a captive, you are free.'

The same day a soldier drove the Greek woman back to Monastir. The carriage driver did not arrive with the note until three days later.

He told Gerasim's family that he had been beaten severely to make him tell who Kyrias was, but assured them he had not, because Gerasim 'was a stranger to him'. He also told them Gerasim had been 'treated with respect, offered coffee and furnished with an extra great coat'.[8]

In *Captured by Brigands*, Gerasim gives a detailed account of the abduction which differs considerably from the driver's story, giving grounds for suspicion. Gerasim makes no mention of the driver being beaten nor of the brigands serving coffee to their captive or treating him 'with respect'. Instead Gerasim recalls asking for a drink only to find the brigands 'not in the least obliging and one of them aimed a blow at me with the butt of his rifle and cursed me'. Also, the driver's purported ignorance of Gerasim's identity seems most unlikely as he was one of only two passengers in the carriage and they had travelled together for hours. However, one fact alone, that the driver slowed the carriage at the ravine near Laithiza and refused to drive the horses any faster, is compelling evidence that he had colluded with the brigands.

Gerasim's family was devastated by the news. Brigandage was a part of life, but kidnapping was normally a fate reserved for the sons of wealthy merchants, not poor tradesmen. It was common knowledge that the victim's sufferings often resulted in death, either during confinement or shortly after release. Dhimiter Kyrias sought help from the missionaries who advised him to report the incident directly to the authorities. He appealed to the vali who assured him there was nothing to fear; his son would certainly be free in five or six days.

Baird was then away on a tour. Jenney and his wife had returned to America the previous year due to illness, to be replaced by another American couple, Lewis and Fanny Bond. Bond went to the Austrian consul, then acting British vice-consul, to express his concern that should it become known the British were involved, Gerasim's foreign connections would be revealed and cause the brigands to increase their demands. In his view it was best for Gerasim's family to handle the negotiations alone and hopefully arrange a modest ransom.

Bond also recommended they wait to inform Thomson of the capture, but Seefried, lacking Bond's sound judgment, sent a telegram to Bible House on 15 November. Thomson immediately telegraphed consul-general Blunt in Thessaloniki, requesting he 'do all possible for Kyrias'.[9] He also sent a message to his Committee in London. Word of the capture was spreading fast.

Blunt shared Bond's views and expressed this opinion in a letter to the ambassador in Istanbul, written on 18 November 1884:

I should indeed be glad if I could be of any service to the Bible Society in this untoward event, but I have considered it my duty in the interest of the unfortunate man, subject to your approval, not to take any official action in the matter. Were the brigands to suspect that we took any active interest in Mr. Kyrias they would undoubtedly claim heavy ransom for his release in the belief that Her Majesty's Government would undertake to pay it.[10]

Back in London, however, the BFBS Committee met to discuss the matter and decided to made a direct appeal to the Foreign Office. As a result, Blunt, despite his reservations, received orders from London to 'endeavour to obtain release and report'.[11] The Turkish authorities now knew that Britain would act on behalf of the captive.

Meanwhile, there was confusion among the brigands. They had taken Gerasim because Shahin had been told he was a rich Vlach merchant carrying 20,000 Turkish lira. When their new prisoner claimed he was from a poor Albanian family, they sent men to Monastir to find his father. They soon returned with the news that Shahin had been deceived.

Having descended Dry Mountain to the plain of Maliq, north of Kortcha, the brigands headed with their captive for the mountains of Opar, the home district of Shahin Matraku. Travelling by night to avoid detection, they crossed rivers, streams and rugged terrain. During the day they kept Gerasim hidden in barns and small slatted huts common to the region or in the woods and hills. For three days they camped out in the ruins of a church in the village of Kutsak, just above Popchishta.

The brigands were amazed by their new captive. Normally their victims cursed, wept or pleaded for mercy. Gerasim did none of these. Instead he told them stories from the Bible and taught them his Albanian hymns. Reports reached Monastir that the brigands had begun to regard Gerasim as 'the most extraordinary man they ever met'.

In one house Gerasim taught a twelve-year-old boy the Lord's Prayer. He later said: 'Gladly would I endure the sufferings of a captive all my life, if I were free to teach my brethren to read, and to gain that knowledge which makes the reader the friend of God, a light among his fellows, and a blessing to his native land'.

For several weeks the brigands continued their flight westward along the Devoll River. They wore *opinga*, a type of leather moccasin well suited to the rugged mountain trails. Gerasim had only the shoes he was captured in and suffered greatly because of them.

One day they descended to the river, crossed it southwards, and climbed another mountain to the village of Zerets. Near this place Gerasim would spend 56 wretched days imprisoned in the house of a man named Yashar. And near this place, a few years later in a *teqe* higher up the mountain, Shahin Matraku would meet his bitter end, betrayed by friends into the hands of his enemies.[12]

Shahin decided to split up the band while they negotiated the ransom. He left two men in charge of the prisoner. As the days dragged into weeks, they grew increasingly anxious and agitated. Blaming Gerasim for their misery, their actions became 'more brutal day by day.' They heated nails in the fire and dropped them down his neck for sport or tossed burning corn husks on his head to set his hair alight. They often struck him 'to pass away the time, for they had nothing else to do'. One day they cut off his beard and rammed beeswax into his ears with sticks to prevent him from overhearing their conversations. He ate only dry bread crusts and water.

And there were aspects to their prisoner that disturbed them. Gerasim writes:

At night, when they lay down to sleep, I went to one side to pray. They understood that I was praying then. This enraged them greatly. Fear came upon them, and it seemed that their conscience troubled them. One of them sputtered and scolded; the other with kicks made me lie down, lest I should keep on praying. Perhaps they thought I was beseeching God to take vengeance on them for all the sufferings they were causing me.

In January the British military attaché, Major Henry Trotter, visited Monastir to inquire into Turkish efforts to find Gerasim. In a show of good will, the vali sent two companies of soldiers into the mountains. This action impressed the Major, but greatly agitated the brigands who became even more embittered against their prisoner. They considered killing him to spare their own lives.

Gerasim's friends and family continued their efforts to save him, but the presence of the soldiers made it impossible to reach his captors.

Shahin had now learned of Gerasim's foreign links and sent a man to make him write another ransom note, this time increasing their demands to 2,500 Turkish lira. Gerasim said: 'But of whom are you asking this money? Why do you strive for so hopeless a thing, and, moreover, complicate me with it?'

The brigand replied: 'Write what we tell you, and give yourself no trouble about the money; the Queen of England will pay it for you, as you are employed by an English company.'

By February Gerasim's guards were very distressed, for zaptiehs often passed through the village. One day, when the beeswax had loosened in his ears, Gerasim overheard their discussions in the next room.

'This fellow has captured us, and he makes our bones to rot, sitting in one place,' said one.

'You are right,' said the other: 'but what can we do? We can't go outside the door with our captive without suffering for it.'

'I say,' replied the first: 'let us kill him outright, and tell the captain that he died.'

Yashar, the owner of the house, said: 'It is not wise to do so, for then we lose all our trouble and the bread on which we have fed him; let us wait a few days more, and then take him away from here, and keep him in the cave in the woods.'

But the brigands were intent upon murdering their captive. 'Unless we kill him, I don't believe we can save ourselves,' said the first.

'How shall we do this?'

'Let us three take an ax apiece, and stand here in the door, and call to him to come out; as soon as he comes out, we each will immediately strike him once or twice, and end him. Then we will put him in a sack and throw him into the river. If we do this, not even the devil will know it.' The other replied: 'I think it better to take him alive down to the river, and there kill him; for should he screech, there is no one there to hear him. Then we'll tie a stone to his waist, and cast him into the river.'

Yashar, determined to prevent them, said: 'Let us wait a few more days: you mustn't wonder that the money hasn't come; it is a hard winter — the roads are blocked with snow. Besides this, who dares to come about this business? A regiment of soldiers have started in pursuit of the captain. We hear that someone sent from England has arrived in Monastir and set the Pasha on fire to find the captive. Have patience a little longer.'

With this and other arguments, Yashar persuaded the brigands to delay their plan.

Then, on 16 February, three zaptiehs entered the village. It was late and they decided to spend the night in Yashar's house. The women of the house scolded them, saying: 'We have no room,' but the zaptiehs entered unbidden, settling into the main room where the family lived. Only a wall now separated them from the captive.

The brigands were terrified and their faces grew pale. Gerasim could feel his heart quicken and his courage return. He did not sleep at all that night, but lay watching and planning his escape:

This was a critical hour for me — either to gain my freedom or die that night. One of these two must happen.

The brigands sat in silence with large knives drawn, but thinking Gerasim was unaware of the presence of the men, they did not threaten him.

Early the next morning he heard the zaptiehs preparing to leave. One of the brigands held the door while the other peered through a hole in the wall. As the zaptiehs descended the stairs, the brigand at the door joined his companion at the wall. Seeing his chance, Gerasim flung himself at the door, caught it in both hands and broke it open. Leaping into the room he shouted for the zaptiehs. The brigands ran after him and the women of the house attacked him savagely, but he fought them off, expecting the zaptiehs to come to his rescue. The women screamed to drown his cries.

In an instant a brigand grabbed him by the throat and the other, with help from the women, caught his legs and he fell. They pinned him to the floor where he could neither breathe nor move. One of the men picked up a knife and pressed the point just below his ear. Gerasim awaited death.

Yashar entered the room to say that the zaptiehs had not learned of Gerasim's presence. Hearing the cries, Yashar had told them his wife had tripped and fallen down the stairs. The men were gone.

The brigands were now 'angry as demons'. They bound Gerasim and dragged him back to his cell where, for the rest of the day, they took turns holding a rope tightly around his neck with a thumb to his windpipe to keep him from calling out. That night they prepared to leave.

They gave Gerasim an old, worn-out pair of *opinga*, which he struggled to tie to his feet. Again they rammed beeswax into his ears and blindfolded him. They dragged him along by a rope around his neck and, unable to see where to put his feet, he often stumbled. He thought they were looking for a place to kill him, but they took him instead to a cave where they kept him for five days. They then moved to a hut for two days before returning to a house where they had been before. Here he lay bound on the floor for 26 days, his eyes covered and his arms tied behind his back. They fed him scraps of food and made him drink water from his *fez*, or thick, felt cap. They struck him with whatever was at hand and mocked him, asking: 'Who hit you?' He did not answer, for they perverted everything he said. They beat him daily.

In London the Foreign Office was growing impatient. On 23 February, consul-general Blunt paid a visit to the vali of Thessaloniki and asked him to remind the vali of Monastir 'that the Provincial authorities would incur great responsibility should they fail to secure the release of Mr. Kyrias.'[13] The next day the vali of Monastir sent this reply:

> With reference to your telegram of today, there is nothing impossible in this world; though the most energetic efforts have not been spared in trying to effect the release

of the man you enquired about, I must inform you that
the desired result has not been attained yet.[14]

However, new revelations regarding the vali's 'energetic efforts'
had brought the missionaries to the brink of despair. They
learned that the military officer in charge of the operation to
free Gerasim was the son-in-law of Alo Bey, a powerful landlord
of Kortcha whom they considered to be in league with most of
the brigands of the country'.[15] Alo Bey was a personal friend of
Shahin Matraku.

On 6 March, Thomson wrote to his friend, Thomas Brown,
of the Turkish Mission Aid Society in London. Their suspicions
of treachery were growing:

It is with deep sorrow that I have to inform you of the
continued captivity of our dear friend, Mr. Kyrias. The
promises of the local authorities as to his speedy deliv-
erance have proved utterly worthless, and though during
the presence at Monastir of Major Trotter, the Military
Attaché of Her Majesty's Embassy, the governor sent a
troop of soldiers in pursuit of the brigands, and pressed
them it appears, rather severely; our confidence in the
success of this pursuit was considerably damped on learning that the commanding officer of the soldiers was son-
in-law to the man who is believed to be the head of all the
brigands in the district.

Another suspicious circumstance, and one which has
given a new and painful aspect to the whole affair, is that
the Greek Bishop of Kortcha is the most intimate friend
of the person already referred to, and who is popularly
regarded as the real governor of all Albania. Hence our
friends at Monastir are coming to the conviction that the

seizure of Mr. Kyrias is really a flagrant case of religious persecution; and I confess I am inclined to agree with them, though there is no direct proof of it. For Mr. Kyrias was well known as an Albanian labouring for the evangelisation of his people through their own mother tongue, a procedure which, for both political and ecclesiastical reasons, the Greek Church has always steadily opposed, and hitherto, alas, but too successfully.[16]

Consul-general Blunt supplied his Embassy with similar information from Baird in Monastir.

I wish only to add that I suppose that either some of the Beys of Kortcha or the Bishop of that place have set up the brigands to increase their original demand fivefold.[17]

On 10 March, Blunt sent a coded telegram to the ambassador, recommending that both Alo Bey and his son-in-law 'be removed from district of Monastir pending negotiations with brigands'.[18] The Sublime Porte passed these instructions on to the vali of Monastir who responded emphatically that 'no such person as Alo Bey is to be found in the Vilayet of Monastir'.[19]

It was obvious the vali had little intention of securing Gerasim's release. But, as the incident threatened to adversely affect Turkish foreign interests, the Minister of Foreign Affairs at the Sublime Porte, Afraim Pasha, took action. The British government was informed that the Minister had 'recourse to certain means which he hopes may lead soon to Mr. Kyrias's release'.[20] Blunt notified Baird of this development, the first hopeful piece of information they had received since the capture.

Ultimately, however, it was the missionaries who were responsible for the difficult decisions and negotiations. It was up to them to find a reliable messenger willing to risk the danger of seeking out the brigands. Tsiku volunteered, but the authorities, acting under the vali's instructions, refused to grant him the necessary travel documents.

Soon after, a Macedonian from Ohrid named Nikola Zarché offered his services. Little did the missionaries realise that their need had exposed them to further intrigue and treachery. Zarché had close links with the leaders of the Greek Orthodox Church. Unaware of this fact, the missionaries accepted Zarché's services. He set off to meet the brigands in the first week of April.

Zarché returned with a letter from Gerasim and a note from Shahin in which the brigands agreed to 700 lira as the final price for the ransom. Five hundred lira, wrote Shahin, could be paid openly in front of the other brigands, but the other 200 lira were to be given secretly to himself and his second-in-command, Nuri.

Gerasim's friends from Samokov, the missionaries in Monastir, and his colleagues at Bible House in Istanbul all contributed generously toward the ransom fund, but it fell to the Bible Society to pay the largest sum. Bond informed Thomson, then in Thessaloniki, of Shahin's demands. Thomson authorised payment of 700 Turkish lira, nearly ten years wages for Gerasim, on 20 April 1885.

Bond tried to persuade the messenger to take another letter offering 450 Turkish lira, but Zarché refused, insisting that 700 lira was the lowest amount the brigands would accept. Shahin had fixed a point beyond Ohrid for payment and the surrender of Kyrias. To ensure the money arrived safely in Ohrid, Bond accepted the Austrian consul's offer to send his best guard and an escort of mounted zaptieh with Zarché to Ohrid.[21]

The brigands began their long march to the exchange place. Gerasim staggered along blindfolded, his clothes in tatters, his flesh exposed. His overcoat was now a useless tangle of rags, worn through from the endless miles he'd trudged along mountain trails and from sleeping rough on the ground. Exhausted and near starvation, Gerasim's hopes waned.

Then, unexpectedly, on 8 April 1885, they removed his blindfold. It was a day he would never forget:

> It had just dawned, but the sun was not up. I felt great joy when I saw the light, after forty days in darkness. I forgot that I was a captive; the brigands seemed like other men.[22]

On the morning of 28 April, they descended a mountain, crossed a deep ravine, and came to a valley. Shahin had now joined them.

They continued to a hill where Zarché was waiting with his younger brother. Zarché unfolded the cloth belt in which he had carried the gold coins and laid it before Shahin.

Counting the money, they found only 300 lira. Shahin said angrily: 'We agreed to seven hundred lira, where are the other four hundred?'

'That's all they gave me,' replied Zarché and began to swear many oaths.

When Shahin asked for the letter from the missionaries, Zarché claimed they had not given him one. Nuri said: 'I am sorry that Kyrias has to suffer much yet, and is not to be ransomed.'

The brigands began discussing the situation among themselves. Some wanted to hold Gerasim until the rest of the money arrived, but most felt he had suffered enough. In the end they decided to release him.

The question of the missing 400 lira was answered in an interesting account from Sevasti's memoirs concerning the Macedonian revolt of 1903. It was autumn and she was returning to Kortcha from Monastir. Her normal route blocked by insurgents, she travelled north to Ohrid instead, intending to continue her journey to Kortcha via another road. In the distance she saw villages burning. From the mountains great pillars of fire lit the night sky. Greatly relieved to reach Ohrid in safety, she made her way to a local inn. Sevasti tells the story:

> The owner and the manager of the hotel, where I spent the night, was a woman. She came to greet me, as she was anxious to get news of the uprising. I told her what was permissible. Seeing that I was reserved, she turned the conversation in another direction. Complaining of the hard times and of the Turkish oppression, she said that she couldn't even earn her daily bread. 'It was quite different when my husband was living!', she said. 'We had plenty of customers and good profits.' During this conversation, I happened to ask her some questions about incidents of previous years and quite innocently she related to me the story of Shahin Matraku, the brigand chief who had captured and kept my brother Gerasim six months in captivity. She told me that her husband had taken the ransom money to Shahin for the release of a certain young man named Kyrias, little knowing that I was his sister and that it was her husband who had

endangered my brother's life, because instead of paying
to Shahin the [700 Turkish lira] as agreed, he had handed
him only 300! With the rest he had built the hotel where
I was spending the night![23]

The brigands led Gerasim to the village of Lin, on the north-
western shore of Lake Ohrid, where his brother and Tsiku sat
waiting. When they met, they wept. Ashamed of his appearance, Gerasim tried to cover himself with the rags of his coat.
He felt like the prodigal son of whom it was said: 'He was dead,
and is alive again; he was lost, and is found'.

Two hours later they went down to the shore of Lake Ohrid
where a boat awaited them. From there they were ferried to
Ohrid and taken to the house of Mr. Zarché where, Gerasim
reported, 'they received us very well'. The next day they
returned to Monastir. His family and friends welcomed him as
one 'returned from the dead'.

His ordeal, which had nearly cost him his life, was finally
over. But rather than now choose an easier, less dangerous path,
Gerasim instead committed himself even more fully to the task
at hand. Alexander Thomson summed up Gerasim's determination with these words:

> After [a full] six month's captivity, Mr. Kyrias was released,
> and this trial, from the view it gave him of the social mis-
> ery of his people, greatly deepened Mr. Kyrias's resolu-
> tion to labour for their evangelization, which he felt to be
> the only sure remedy.[24]

The time had come to push back the gates. A new day was
dawning for Albania.

Kayo (centre, with beard), one of the brigands who captured Gerasim in 1884. Photo courtesy of Richard Cochrane.

A small slatted hut in Shahin Matraku's village of Popqishta,
typical of the type Gerasim was held in during his capture.

View of Lake Ohrid and the village of Lin
from where Gerasim was released from captivity in 1885.

CHAPTER 7

HARVEST FIELDS

IN HIS ABSENCE, GERASIM'S duties had been shared between
Monastir and Istanbul, with Thomson directing the colporteurs
and Bond keeping the books. Upon his return, Gerasim once
again took charge of his field and set about putting things in order. Tsiku's sales were thriving and Jovancho too had proved himself capable. Seefried, on the other hand, continued to do poorly.

In September 1885, George began his studies at the
American Theological Institute of Samokov. Gerasim resumed
teaching Albanian reading and grammar to his sister and three
other Albanian pupils of the American Mission's girls' school.
A young shoemaker also came to his house three times a week.
By December Gerasim was teaching Albanian to ten students.
He told Thomson of their work:

> I wrote you lately, about my Albanian class. Now I teach
> them the history of the Old Testament, and, at the same
> time, they prepare Albanian compositions on different
> subjects — once a week. Besides this, I deliver — once
> a week — a lecture on Albanian history, which I gather
> from different books.[1]

British government involvement in his release had yet again brought the work of the Bible Society to the attention of the Sublime Porte. More difficulties might have arisen had not the Grand Vizier, Sait Pasha, fallen from grace. In September 1885, the Bulgarians, through political intrigue and military action, succeeded in annexing the vast territory of East Rumelia, today Bulgaria south of the Balkan Mountains. Blaming this loss on his Grand Vizier, the Sultan removed him from office. The man who had so vigorously resisted the Albanian work was gone.

Nevertheless, there were other obstacles to overcome. The unsettled state of the country and the constant threat of unrest had caused economic and social instability. In his annual report to the BFBS Committee for 1886, Thomson described the terrible reality of 'the pomp and circumstance of glorious war', a reality seldom reflected in the newspapers and periodicals of the day:

> The agitation of men's minds, the pressure of taxation, the interruption of trade and industry, and too often a relaxed condition of both faith and morals, not to mention cases of individual suffering, combine to render war, in almost every case, the greatest calamity which can befall a nation.

Gerasim worked on despite the difficulties. Impressed by his abilities, Thomson commended him to the committee in London with 'hearty approbation for the diligence and care with which he has discharged his duties, and especially for his judicious marking out of tours for the colporteurs under his direction'.[2] Gerasim kept an eye on the many semi-autonomous, independent villages and districts that had never before been visited and planned the colporteur's tours with the spirit of a strategist. 'It would be wonderful indeed', wrote Thomson, 'yet not without parallel in many instances, should the Gospel find admission into strongholds, which the whole power of the government has been unable to subdue'.[3]

In June Gerasim resumed his Albanian service. He reported to Thomson:

> You know Monastir is an important key to all Albania, and many Albanians from Kortcha and elsewhere visit this town. In the inns, where they remain for a few days, they are told that there is Albanian preaching here, and having tried, they have found the place and attended our meetings. During the last year, many hearers from Albania, mostly from Kortcha, have heard the Gospel preached. So the words of life have gone quietly, and influenced a good many Albanians. Last Sunday, three persons from Kortcha attended the preaching and were greatly satisfied. They had never heard any preaching before. I am told that they were so pleased to hear the Gospel in their own language, that they are impatiently waiting the next Sunday to hear the Gospel preached again.[4]

For Gerasim, Albania had two primary needs. First was for the gospel to be proclaimed in Albanian throughout the country, and second, for the establishment of Albanian schools where the debilitating chains of ignorance and superstition could be broken as the children were taught in their mother tongue.

Regarding Albanian in the church, the historical development of the two Christian traditions in Albania, Greek Orthodoxy in the south and Roman Catholicism in the north, until that time had been such that neither encouraged the use of the Albanian language for liturgical or devotional purposes. Among other races and peoples, for example the Slavic tribes to the east, early Christian missionaries such as Cyril and Methodius had used the language of the people to express the message of Christianity. They translated the scriptures into the vernacular and as a result large numbers converted to Christ. Out of their work grew strong national expressions of Christian faith. In Albania, however, from time immemorial the language of the Church had been either Latin or Greek. Not only were the people left in ignorance, but the priests themselves often did not understand the words they recited. Gerasim longed for his people to hear the message of Jesus Christ. Of the gospel in Albania he wrote:

> The words of life which enlighten hearts, bring joy and lead to the right path, have unfortunately been hidden from our eyes up until this day. Few are those who understand the sweetness and power of the words of the gospel. But if the lessons of the gospel are so valuable, why should they not be read in Albanian in the churches of Albania, for everyone to understand? If we wish to bring civilization, goodness and days of blessing to Albania, these lessons must be sown in every heart, so that the oldest and the youngest might know them. These lessons will bring us love and fellowship, for they teach us to love not only our friends, but also our enemies, they make us faithful in every deed, they save us from the discontent and hatred that are found in our midst, and lead us to prosper in every good work, for ourselves and for others.[5]

However, and as is so often the case for the reformer, Gerasim's intentions were perceived as a threat by the religious establishment of his day. The development of an Albanian-speaking Christian community ran contrary to their interests and they strongly opposed him. As long as he lived, Gerasim remained a focus for their animosity and hatred.

As for Albanian schools, various societies were organised in the late nineteenth century to plan and encourage their development. The 'Istanbul Committee', which began with the Frasheri brothers and Yani Vreto, Koto Hoxho and others, had established 'The Society for the Publication of Albanian Literature' in 1879. The work soon expanded with affiliates in Bucharest and Alexandria. In 1884 the Bucharest branch became an independent society called *Drita* (Light), which set up a press to print textbooks and other materials beyond the reach of the Ottoman government. The *Drita* Society of Bucharest also developed its own Latin-based alphabet, which they proposed for all future Albanian publications in both dialects. However, the difficult question of a single alphabet for Albanian would not be resolved until the 'Congress of Monastir' in 1908.

Thomson regarded these attempts to devise a single alphabet for Albanian as a very positive development, though he preferred to wait until one alphabet found general acceptance among the populace before using it in the Bible Society's publications. This was in no way from a desire to maintain a division between Gheg and Tosk Albanians as has been purported by some Albanian historians. The BFBS had been publishing literature in Albanian since the 1820s, long before anyone else, and had developed a two-alphabet system in order to enable as many Albanians as possible to read the scriptures. This was, however, only a temporary solution. Concerning national unity Thomson's opinion was clear: '...when once there are national schools, there should be only one alphabet for the whole nation'.[6]

But now, while the Bible Society's permission to print in Tosk was still valid, they prepared two single gospels in August 1885, again in the Greek alphabet. Pandeli Sotiri, an Albanian linguist whom Gerasim had first met during his stay in Istanbul in 1884 and who had served as editor for the Istanbul Committee's periodical, *Dituria*, was hired to correct the press.[7]

In Albania the work expanded rapidly under Gerasim's direction. He recommended that George Thoshe, a thirty-year-old Vlach, be sent to Shkodra. Thomson, who had long wanted to re-establish a work in the city, was delighted and sailed there with Thoshe in May 1886. Seefried too made the journey, travelling overland from Monastir. Preceding Thomson to Shkodra by a week, Seefried began to make public the purpose of their visit. In response the Roman Catholic clergy, who were suspicious of the Bible Society and very influential in Shkodra,

filled the minds of the great mass of the Christian population with alarm and jealousy, as if our object had been to offer violence in the least degree to the religious convictions of anyone. Not satisfied with this... they petitioned the vali to forbid your Agent opening a Depot or establishing colporteurs there for the dissemination of the word of God.[8]

When Thomson arrived and called on the vali of Shkodra, the official stated categorically that the Bible Society could neither open a depot nor sell even a single book until orders arrived from Istanbul. Knowing it would take weeks to settle the question, Thomson drew up a statement for the consideration of the Sublime Porte explaining that the Bible Society merely intended to resume a work which it had previously carried on for eight years in Shkodra, 'without offence to anyone, as many of the citizens could testify'.[9] He then departed, leaving Thoshe and Seefried behind.

Months after his return to the capital, the Porte denied Thomson's request to sell scriptures in Shkodra, but nonetheless ordered the books to be returned to the colporteurs. In the intervening months, however, the alarm of the people in Shkodra had passed away. According to Thomson, Seefried and Thoshe 'had won golden opinions for the Society and the vali saw that he could without danger permit the circulation of the Scriptures'.[10] Giving yet another example of Ottoman inconsistency, the vali allowed the men to sell. In December 1886, Gerasim went to Shkodra to help set up the depot.

There were now five men under Gerasim's direction disseminating Albanian literature throughout the Albanian territories from three centres: Shkodra, Skopje and Monastir.

The colporteurs often worked under very difficult conditions. Life in European Turkey at the end of the nineteenth century could be extremely harsh and some of the men lost loved ones to sickness and disease. Brigandage was also rife and, travelling by foot or mule on open roads, they were often exposed to danger. Throughout the vilayets local authorities continued to mete out 'rough justice' and the bishops grew increasingly vindictive, at times enticing local populations to violence against the Society's workers. A colporteur had to rely on his wits to succeed or even survive.

One day in 1887, Tsiku visited Discata, a village of some 700 houses in southern Albania. Early in the morning, he went to the *muhtar*, or village mayor, who examined his books and papers. Finding everything in order, the muhtar permitted Tsiku to sell and he soon gathered a large crowd. Hearing of this, the local bishop sent two teachers to prohibit the villagers from purchasing the books. Tsiku gathered his supplies and went to the bishop to ask that the 'poor, simple people who were hungering and thirsting for the Word of Life' be allowed to buy. The bishop adamantly refused and went to the muhtar demanding that Tsiku be immediately expelled from the village. The muhtar summoned Tsiku publicly and told him before the crowd that because the bishop 'complained of his books being of an injurious nature, he could not be allowed to sell them, and must leave the place'. Tsiku refused, reminding the muhtar he had earlier declared the books to be in order. He then turned to the bishop and challenged him to point out any error in the Bible Society's translations, adding 'if they did not in every respect agree with the scriptures read in the Orthodox Church, he would himself be the first to burn them'. The bishop admitted they were the same, but explained to the muhtar that the Church did not want the colporteurs to come and sell them to the people.

> The muhtar saw that the bishop had made an important admission, but for peace sake again urged Tsiku to quit the place. But the latter replied: 'You know that my passport and books are in perfect order, and I cannot consent to depart without a written order from you to do so.' On this the muhtar turned to the bishop and said:

'Unless your Holiness give me a written request to send
away this man, I cannot be responsible for doing so, seeing he has the government seal on his books, and has
been allowed to sell them by other governors all over
the country.' The bishop was too prudent to give any
such document, and so, to the great discomfiture of the
bishop and the two teachers, but to the joy of the villagers who crowded around, the muhtar told Tsiku that he
was at perfect liberty to go and sell as many books as he
could.[11]

Thus Kristoforidhi's translations of the scriptures and copies of
his grammar and other Albanian books came into the hands
of Albanians across the nation, and many learned to read their
mother tongue.

Gerasim's numerous responsibilities, directing the colporteurs, keeping accounts, overseeing the depot, dealing with the
authorities, preparing literature for the press and more, left him
with little time to himself. But as he approached his twenty-
ninth birthday, he turned his attention to matters of a more
personal nature. Now earning a regular income, though not a
large salary, he considered his prospects for marriage. With this
purpose in mind, he visited Samokov in July 1887. Thomson
offered his advice in choosing a 'help-meet:'

Of course the first thing in selection of a partner is true
piety, and next, fitness for the particular sphere she would
be called to occupy. She would need to learn, if possible,
the Albanian language, and have a sympathy with the
people in their love of liberty and their historical songs
and ballads, but far more in seeking to teach especially

the women and girls to read and to understand what the
gospel really is. She would need to be one who would
interest herself in the religious instruction of her sex
among the Albanian people, and who would think such
work more truly honourable and enjoyable, than the
society of the frivolous and ungodly, however rich and
honoured.[12]

Gerasim was engaged to a Miss Klonares from Samokov, a
girl whose father had worked for the American Bible Society,
though not a man whom Thomson held in high regard. They
planned to be married the following year.

He returned to Monastir in festive mood with his brother,
George, who was to spend several weeks during the summer
break colporting for the Bible Society. Yani Marmaroff, a close
friend and classmate at Samokov, also joined George on his
tours.

In October 1887, Gerasim again visited Kortcha where he was
now highly regarded. The Bucharest Committee, through Naim
Frasheri's considerable influence in the Ministry of Education,
had managed to secure an *irade*, or imperial permission, to open
the first Albanian school for boys in Kortcha. The irade had been
issued in the name of Pandeli Sotiri, Gerasim's friend from his
time in Istanbul. Pandeli now served as director for the new
school that used a house generously supplied for this purpose by
Diamand Tërpo, a member of the Bucharest Committee.

One of the biggest challenges facing the boys' school was the
need for textbooks in Albanian. Sami and Naim Frasheri, Yani
Vreto and others worked to prepare books in subjects such as
history, science and geography as well as an Albanian grammar,

all of which were printed on the Bucharest Society's printing press between 1886 and 1888.

Gerasim enjoyed the opportunity to renew his contact with Pandeli and stayed on in Kortcha for several weeks. Each Sunday he was allowed to use the new schoolhouse, or *Mësonjtorja* as it was called, a powerful symbol in the struggle for independence, for his Albanian worship services. Large numbers attended these meetings. Three times a week he gave Bible instruction at the school and taught the pupils his Albanian hymns.

> This not only delighted the children, but proved to be a powerful attraction to their parents and friends, many of whom attended the Bible-lessons in the school. A choir of the pupils sang these hymns at public worship, and strong men's eyes were filled with tears at hearing their own children sing sweet gospel hymns in their own language, which had been for so many centuries proscribed as profane and incapable of properly expressing divine truth. Not only so, some at least seemed to be deeply impressed with the truth preached, and urged him to return speedily and water the seed he had sown. He was even requested to send a weekly sermon, which the teacher might read to them, in a meeting for praise.[13]

During his stay Gerasim became convinced that the time had come to establish a Protestant church in Kortcha.[14] When he returned to Monastir in December 1887, he spoke with the missionaries about being ordained for this purpose. Gerasim now thought Kortcha best suited as a base for the central headquarters of the Albanian work. Thomson was very encouraged and expressed his hope that Kortcha might become 'the best foundation for Bible work and national reform'.[15]

Another issue demanding his attention concerned Sevasti's future. Her school days were coming to an end and, according to Albanian custom, she would soon be kept in seclusion until the family could arrange for her marriage. But Sevasti now embraced her own hopes and dreams. Over the years Gerasim had carefully followed her progress at the American school in Monastir and told her stories from his travels in Albania, describing the life and conditions of the children there. When he reported the excitement surrounding the establishment of the new school for boys, Sevasti knew she too must dedicate her life to teaching her people. Fully aware that such a task required further preparation, Gerasim applied on her behalf to the American Mission's College for Women in Istanbul.

Some months later a letter arrived from the college, which should have been cause for celebration. She had been accepted into the class of 1888. But when they broke the news to their family, Sevasti instead found herself in a serious conflict with her parents who staunchly refused to break with tradition in this matter. To them it was inconceivable for a young, unmarried girl to leave her home and move to a foreign city, whatever the purpose or however noble the cause. And as to education, for them Sevasti had already received far more than a woman could ever use. The time had come for her to be married.

For three months the battle raged as Dhimiter and Maria held their ground until at last they capitulated in exasperation before their determined offspring. Sevasti later wrote, 'this long fight to break the custom of seclusion helped me to see clearly just what I was to do when through with my studies'.[16] It was not going to be easy to persuade Albanian families to commit themselves to their daughters' education.

In the autumn of 1888, Sevasti would pack her things and leave for Istanbul, accompanied by Lewis Bond and several other girls from their school in Monastir. Sevasti would become the first Albanian woman ever to earn a college diploma.

At the same time as Gerasim urged his parents to think in new ways for their daughter, he also managed to persuade Thomson that the Bible Society should begin using the new alphabet of the Bucharest committee for their Albanian publications. Such a decision, which involved the substantial financial implications of typesetting and new print runs, however, would require the approval of the Committee in London. Thomson presented them with Gerasim's arguments in a detailed letter written on 3 May 1888.[17] The Committee approved the request and Gerasim spent much of the summer of 1888 transcribing Kristoforidhi's translation of the gospel of Matthew into the new letters.

In August 1888, Gerasim returned to Samokov for his wedding with Miss Klonares, but events now took an unexpected and embarrassing turn. When he arrived he learned his fiancée had come to the conclusion, rather late, that a life in Albania among the Albanians was not for her. The wedding was called off and Gerasim returned, alone, to Monastir.

Though he expressed relief for not having 'married one whose heart was only half in the work of the Lord', Gerasim now found himself in debt to the Society. Apart from the many expenses incurred by a Balkan engagement, he was also supporting his family who were hard-pressed having lost an additional wage with George away at Samokov. He requested an increase in salary, which was denied, though the Committee did agree to give him ten pounds sterling to help him through his difficulties.

One month after his return from Samokov, on 18 September 1888, a Sunday evening as he was preparing to travel to Bucharest to oversee the printing of Matthew in the new letters, several zaptiehs arrived at his house and demanded to enter the depot. Gerasim began arguing furiously with them. Fifty years later Sevasti still remembered it as having been 'a hot discussion'. Gerasim objected to their coming on the Lord's Day, and refused to allow anything to be removed from the depot. The zaptiehs could do nothing but seal the building and return the next morning. Arriving early, they confiscated papers and correspondence of every description, books, accounts, and also Gerasim's transcribed manuscript of Matthew.[18]

Gerasim immediately reported the seizure to the British vice-consul, Howard Shipley, who had been assigned to Monastir earlier that year. Since his arrival Shipley had been on friendly terms with Gerasim and the Americans, a fact which deeply disturbed the Greek consul at Monastir who accused Shipley of 'patronizing anti-hellenists, especially missionaries'.[19]

Shipley met with the vali and was able to get the accounts and other books returned, including the manuscript of Matthew, but not Gerasim's letters and correspondence. In addition, the vali informed Gerasim he could not leave Monastir till he be 'freed from all suspicion'.[20] No charge was ever brought against him, nor any reason given for these actions, but months passed before Gerasim was permitted to travel again.

During Gerasim's detention in Monastir, the country returned to a more peaceful state. Thomson wrote in his annual report for 1889:

'The war-clouds that darkened the horizon, for a time, began to disperse'. But we are thankful that, for the most part, your agents have been free to go forth in the name of the Lord to cope with ignorance, error, prejudice and fanaticism, and even persecution. Of such things we cannot complain: their prevalence and power are the very reason for that grand Commission itself, which is changing the face of the world, and which our ascending Lord gave to his disciples: — 'Go ye therefore and teach all nations, — and, lo, I am with you always, even unto the end of the world.' It is because we regard the operations of the Bible Society as an essential part of the work entrusted to the Church, that we feel it to be a holy service, eminently involving the glory of God and the salvation of men, and in the prosecution of which every faithful worker may confidently reckon on the presence and support of his divine Lord.[21]

Gerasim spent these months transcribing the Psalms into the new letters and overseeing the colporteurs. He also hired a new colporteur, Christos Shoulis, a native of Kortcha, to visit the mountain villages around his hometown.[22]

As a result of the increased circulation of Albanian scriptures there was growing demand among Orthodox Albanians for the use of Albanian in their liturgy. In August 1888, British consul-general Blunt in Thessaloniki sent his Embassy a copy of a letter to the Ecumenical Patriarch of Constantinople, Dionysius, in which leading Orthodox Albanians expressed this desire.[23] But similar concessions in Bulgaria had lead to a schism and the creation of an independent Bulgarian Orthodox Church in 1870. Determined to prevent such a development in Albania at all costs, the Patriarch denied their request. Decades would pass before the establishment of an Albanian-speaking Orthodox Church could be realised.

The Turkish authorities in Macedonia now intensified their campaign against the Bible Society. The vali of Monastir, with Greek support, seemed resolved to render 'all colportage so difficult and so costly, that the Bible Society shall be compelled to discontinue it'.[24]

While Greek and Turk sought to stifle Albanian aspirations, the number of young Albanians determined to serve their nation was growing. Sevasti Kyrias excelled at her college in Istanbul and in 1889 Fanka Efthimi of Monastir entered the girls' school at Samokov. That same year George Kyrias began his final term and another promising student, Gregor Tsilka, most likely drawn by Gerasim's preaching, also entered Samokov.

At the end of April 1889, after seven long months, the travel ban on Gerasim was finally lifted. He made immediate plans to print Matthew and the Psalms in Bucharest, but in the interim Thomson had met with Naim Frasheri, then head of the Censor's office in Istanbul, who told him not to print the Psalms. 'Print rather the book of Genesis', he said: 'with the history of Creation and the flood, and the Patriarchs. That will be a much better School-book.' Thomson agreed, and Gerasim began transcribing Genesis.[25]

Gerasim left for Bucharest at the end of May, travelling by way of Thessaloniki and Istanbul. Once there he employed Yani Vreto, a leading figure in the Albanian national movement and member of the Bucharest Committee, to help him correct the press. They printed 5,000 copies of Matthew and Genesis. As they worked together the depth of Gerasim's religious convictions surprised and disturbed Vreto. Viewing religion as a potentially divisive force, Vreto, who was from an Orthodox family, later accused Gerasim of introducing a 'new wolf', that is Protestant faith, to Albania.[26] Here again is strong evidence refuting the idea that Gerasim merely espoused Protestantism as a pretext to gain foreign favour. Having worked closely with Gerasim over several months Vreto knew well Gerasim's position on the matter as well as his plans for Albania, and he ardently opposed them.

Gerasim vigorously refuted Vreto on this issue, arguing that as one who lived and worked among the people he was in a better position to understand their needs than those who remained far from the troubled borders of the motherland. Nor did other prominent leaders share Vreto's opinion. Nikolla Naço, president of the Bucharest Committee and editor of the Albanian periodical, *Drita* (Light), supported Gerasim and spoke highly of the Bible Society's contribution to Albania. Though not himself a Protestant, he would one day apply to join an evangelical society established by Gerasim. In letter to the BFBS President in London, Naço expressed his gratitude for the Society's efforts to 'educate and evangelize the Albanian people'.[27]

During his months in Bucharest, Gerasim also suffered continual bouts of fever and discomfort, a portentous sign of the disease that was to take his life. Having finished printing Genesis and Matthew in the new letters in October, he left, still unwell, for Monastir, stopping briefly at Istanbul and Thessaloniki.

Gerasim once again considered his prospects for marriage. The girl this time was Athena Michaelides, daughter of Stavros Michaelides, the former superintendent of the Bible Society's depot in Yanina and now pastor of the Protestant church in

Thessaloniki. Gerasim had met Athena and her family on his
way to Bucharest in May, and revisited them again in October.
Educated in Athens, Athena was bright, dedicated, and willing
to live and work in Albania. Before he departed for Monastir,
they spoke of engagement.

The Committee in London had now approved his request
to move the Bible Society's Albanian headquarters to Kortcha,
so when he arrived in Monastir he quit the depot and moved in
with his father. His friends in Kortcha were 'very anxious' for
him to come and looked forward to his support and encouragement.

In October 1889 Faik Pasha, formerly vali of Kosova, was
installed as the new vali of Monastir.[28] Gerasim hoped this
change might bring an easing of the stringent restrictions lev-
ied against their work, but it was not to be. Faik Pasha would
instead prove to be one of the most fervent and effective opponents of the Bible Society's work in Albania.

Albanians everywhere received copies of Matthew and
Genesis in the new alphabet with great enthusiasm. A sense of
national feeling was clearly spreading among the people. Each
Sunday in Monastir Gerasim's Albanian service was filled to
capacity.

When land was purchased for the Protestant church in Monastir, Gerasim looked forward to the day when they would build
the first Albanian church in Albania. He wrote Thomson: 'If God
helps us to have a church of living stones, the other is easy'.[29]

Gerasim travelled via Thessaloniki in December 1889 on
his way to Shkodra. He had decided to take the easier route
of sailing from Thessaloniki around southern Greece and then
northwards along Albania's Adriatic coast, rather than the tiring

and potentially dangerous overland journey through Kortcha and Berat. It also gave him another opportunity to visit Athena and her family. On 7 December 1889, the young couple were engaged. The next day he sailed for Athens.

His ship was caught in a terrible storm near the island of Skopelos. As the waves crashed violently over the deck Gerasim began to fear the 'fate of the prophet Jonah' for not having taken the direct overland route to Shkodra. He arrived in Athens shaken but grateful where he was warmly welcomed by his future brother-in-law, the renowned Greek Protestant preacher, Xenophon Moschou. On Sunday Gerasim attended the Protestant church where he enjoyed hearing Moschou preach on Jesus' parable of the prodigal son.[30]

Gerasim arrived at the port of Durres on 20 December to find that Thoshe was sick in Fier.[31] Suffering himself with fever, he made his way to Shkodra where there was no one to meet him. Earlier that year Seefried had been caught embezzling Bible Society funds and was dismissed. Gerasim toured the city, preaching in shops and homes, reporting to Thomson that people listened 'with delight' as he read to them from the Gheg Psalms.[32]

He soon realised Thoshe and Seefried, being foreigners, had only worked with those who knew Italian. Gerasim now saw clearly how important it was for the colporteurs to have a knowledge of the local languages, especially Albanian, if they were to accomplish anything. He was also convinced they had little time to lose.

The face of European Turkey was changing rapidly and Albania's future hung in the balance. As the year and the decade came to a close, Gerasim was aware of the significance of his task and how much remained to be done. His song, *Detyrat e mëmëdhetarit të vërtet* (Duties of a True Patriot), reveals the force of his resolve to labour for his people as he implores others to join him in the work:

> *Do punonj për mëmëdhenë:*
> *Gjithë jetën sa të rronj,*
> *Do të zgjonj dhe ata që flenë,*
> *Kështu jetën do mbaronj.*

> *O vëllezër shqipëtarë,*
> *Merrni sot udhën'e mbarë,*
> *Punën tuaj mos harroni,*
> *Koha shkon dhe prapë s'vjen.*

> To toil for the land of my birth,
> As long as this body draws breath;
> To rouse those who sleep unconcerned:
> This my goal till the day of my death.

> O sons of the eagle, my brothers!
> Begin from today the good path;
> To work, do not tire! —
> Time's passing, and never returns.

'This was the oath', wrote Skender Luarasi, 'this was the creed of the patriot, the pedagogue, the renowned Albanian illuminist from Monastir, who, in everything he believed not only preached, but was himself first to begin and to do. The whole life and work of Gerasim Kyrias was a shining example to all the Albanians of the National Awakening'.[33]

CHAPTER 8

SACRED VOWS

THERE WAS MUCH TO encourage Gerasim as he considered his field in 1890. In just five years the nature of the Albanian work had changed dramatically. National sentiment was on the rise. Colporteurs now conducted regular tours throughout the Albanian territories. George, Sevasti, Fanka Efthimi and Gregor Tsilka were all pursuing their studies and Gerasim was about to be married and ordained as a missionary to his people. Yet many difficulties remained. Of primary concern was their lack of finances. And what of their enemies who harassed and resisted them every step of the way?

In Samokov George was facing problems with the Bulgarian authorities. The Bulgarian army, in need of fresh recruits, had begun conscripting young Ottomans studying in Bulgaria. George and his friend, Yani Marmaroff, were told they would be drafted upon graduation. The young men appealed for protection from the Turkish consul in Samokov but to no avail. And so in February 1890, unwilling to serve a foreign country, George and Yani left Samokov without completing their course of study. Consul-general Blunt in Thessaloniki reported to the ambassador that such blatant injustice on the part of the

Bulgarian government was 'causing irritation among the Slavic speaking population of Macedonia'.[1]

Gerasim remained in Shkodra until the end of February 1890, though ill health prevented him from accomplishing much. He was deeply disappointed by what he had seen of Thoshe's work.

The day of his wedding was fast approaching. Gerasim had planned to travel overland to Monastir through Berat and Kortcha but, still weak from fever, he chose instead to return by sea.

On 1 March 1890, he sailed from Durres to Vlora from where another steamer was scheduled to continue to Corfu a few days later. Upon arrival in Vlora he inquired after a suitable place to hold meetings and was offered the use of a room by a young man from Monastir who was living there. Gerasim spent the rest of the day inviting people to come and, on 3 March, preached to an audience of twenty. The following day twenty-eight Albanians filled the room and others crowded outside in the courtyard. Many stayed to talk with him afterwards.

Gerasim took his books to the local kaymakam for inspection. The man was an Albanian and had Gerasim read to him from the Bible for over an hour and a half. Two zaptiehs later visited Gerasim and asked that he read to them also. When he finished they pleaded with him to stay in Vlora for at least a month. The young man from Monastir readily offered the use of his room if only Gerasim would remain.[2] Amazed by their openness, Gerasim must have wondered at the contrast to his first tour in Albania.

A violent storm prevented the steamer from docking for three days. Gerasim used the time to preach and receive visitors. He sailed from Vlora on 8 March, much encouraged, arriving in Athens four days later where he stayed again with Moschou before sailing on to Thessaloniki on 15 March.

Thomson meanwhile had agreed to hire George for Shkodra to share the work with Thoshe, but Gerasim hoped to find another mission to support his brother to help him organise the church in Kortcha. He desperately needed George for preaching, teaching, and other missionary work.[3]

George received a telegram from Thomson directing him to go from Monastir to Shkodra but, as there were no muleteers for hire then, Bond sent him instead to Thessaloniki to sail from there. When Gerasim arrived in Thessaloniki, he was pleasantly surprised to find George waiting for him. With the date of the wedding set for 24 March, there were many preparations to make.

An unusual extravagance also had arrived for Gerasim in Thessaloniki. It was a 'Magic Lantern' from London for which he had paid eleven pounds sterling, nearly two months wages. The lantern was an early form of slide projector, which burned kerosene fuel, reflecting the light through specially prepared glass slides, thus casting a colourful, enlarged image of the picture on the wall. Gerasim was sure such an invention would attract much attention in the villages of Albania, but it took him several tries and a few smoke-filled rooms before he could get it to work properly.

Gerasim asked Thomson to come and perform the marriage ceremony, but shortly before the wedding Thomson's son-in-law died unexpectedly, leaving his daughter alone with four children. Thomson would have to remain in Istanbul.

On the evening of 24 March 1890, before a small gathering of friends and family Gerasim and Athena were married at the

Protestant church of Thessaloniki by Scottish missionary, Peter Crosbie.

Within days George boarded a steamer for Athens and Shkodra while Gerasim and Athena took a train to Gradsko from where they continued by carriage to Monastir.

In April 1890, the European Turkey Mission held its Annual Meeting in Monastir. Thomson accompanied his son, Robert, who was a member of the mission, to participate in the service at which Gerasim would be ordained as evangelist to the Albanian people.

Many gathered for the special ceremony, including members of Gerasim's family. After a public examination the missionaries unanimously agreed to his ordination and, laying their hands on him, prayed a prayer of consecration 'in the presence of a large and deeply interested audience'.[4]

Two weeks later, after just five weeks of marriage, Gerasim and Athena boarded a carriage loaded with their belongings and headed for Kortcha.

The battle lines were about to be redrawn.

Gerasim and Athena Kyrias, ca. 1890

CHAPTER 9

INTO THE FRAY

THEY ARRIVED IN KORTCHA on Saturday, 3 May 1890, and were immediately requested to hold a public worship service the next day. It proved impossible to make all the necessary arrangements so the meeting was postponed until the following Sunday. During the week they settled into their new home and received many 'pleasant encouragements' from the towns-people. News of their arrival spread quickly.

The trustees of the Albanian school insisted that Gerasim hold his Protestant services in their schoolhouse, the *Mësonjtorja*. Gerasim ordered extra benches to seat the anticipated crowds, but no one was prepared for the vast numbers that would actually come.[1]

One week after their arrival, Gerasim visited the mutasarrif of Kortcha. It was a 'pleasant' meeting and he was impressed by the mutasarrif whom he described as 'a wise man'. Gerasim explained to him the work of the Bible Society, the extent of its activity worldwide, and his purpose in coming to Kortcha. The mutasarrif raised no objections.

The next day, Sunday, 11 May 1890, was unprecedented in the history of Kortcha. Four hundred Albanians, men, women and children, crowded into the two large classrooms of the Mësonjtorja to sing Albanian hymns, pray, and hear Gerasim preach in their own language despite 'the strict preventative measures of the Greek clergy'.[2] Just one third of those gathered found seats and several benches broke under the strain. Forty people sat in the windows which remained open so those standing outside could hear.

The school children, accompanied by Athena on a pump organ, sang two hymns that Gerasim had taught them on his earlier visits. Gerasim then preached from the fourth chapter of the Gospel of John about Jesus' encounter with the woman at the well. He told of the Lord's promise to give living water to anyone who desired it, and that it would become in them 'a spring of water welling up to eternal life' (Jn 4:14). For many it was the first time they had ever heard the teachings of Christ in their own language.

The main message at the Greek Orthodox church that morning had been about the arrival of 'the heretics'. With the bishop away in Permet, it fell to the deacon to issue a public statement against Gerasim and Athena. He spoke at length, denouncing them as false teachers whose sole aim was to destroy the faith of the holy fathers.

But far from deterring his flock, the deacon's talk had the opposite effect, rousing even greater curiosity in the newcomers. As a result, attendance at the Protestant meeting was 'larger than that of the Church', a fact which further incensed the Greek leadership. For the rest of the week they levelled bitter complaints and accusations against Gerasim at the office of the mutasarrif. Aware of these actions, Gerasim told Thomson, wryly, that the Greeks were 'disappointed with our coming to Kortcha'.[3] The battle, however, had just begun.

The numbers at the Albanian service surprised everyone. One of the trustees of the school expressed concern about possible damage to the building, but all of them wanted the meetings to continue there. To raise funds for 'new benches and for repairs', Gerasim organised a special presentation with his Magic Lantern.[4]

The mutasarrif, too, had been alarmed by the size of the crowd. When 300 came the next Sunday, he yielded to the demands of an increasingly agitated Greek party, and had Gerasim's house searched and his books and papers confiscated.[5] But house searches and seizures were nothing new to Gerasim. Determined for his work not to be restricted yet again, he sent a telegram to Thomson requesting help. Thomson contacted the Embassy, but the ambassador, William White, though 'active and capable', showed little interest in assisting the Bible Society. Thomson wrote Gerasim:

> I got your telegram, and thank you for it, but I could do nothing without minute information, & only when consuls and consul-generals have done all they could, & failed, can we apply to the ambassador. I hope Mr. Shipley will speak for you to the Vali of Monastir and say that the crowds were merely from curiosity & will soon fall off, and that you did nothing to bring so great a crowd, but wished simply to preach the Gospel. I hope Mr. Bond too will use his influence to get such a prohibition set aside, though no doubt the Greeks will fight hard against us.[6]

However, when the mutasarrif found nothing incriminating or subversive, he returned everything to Gerasim and allowed him to continue his work. Thomson observed,

> We may be thankful that the mutasarrif of Kortcha is a more honest and just man than the Vali of Monastir, who kept you in suspense for a whole year, whereas he, declared you free from suspicion within a week. I rejoice also in the multitudes that attend your service, and hope the Word may prove like an arrow in their hearts, to give them no peace till they come to Jesus for pardon & reconciliation.[7]

In the Greek church, warnings and accusations were read out against Gerasim and the Bible Society with increasing regularity. Thomson advised him to bear it all with patience, 'for', he wrote, 'such falsehoods will do themselves more harm than us'.

Frustrated by the mutasarrif's unwillingness to intervene, the Greeks took their grievances to the vali of Monastir, hoping to find a more sympathetic official. They were not disappointed. In June the vali ordered the mutasarrif of Kortcha to forbid the use of the schoolhouse for Albanian worship. Without funds to hire another hall, Gerasim had no choice but to hold the meetings in his house. After this, the numbers attending were greatly reduced.

Meanwhile in Shkodra, George was suffering from fever and rheumatism and had grown discouraged. Thoshe showed little interest in the work, repeatedly delaying his tours and instead building up a dental practice in the city. Thomson warned him to resume selling or face dismissal. In July 1890, the Committee in London decided to let him go. George's former classmate, Yani

Marmaroff, who remained in Monastir, was sent to Shkodra to replace him.

At this time colporteur Christos Shoulis met with an unfortunate tragedy in Kortcha. One of his children died and, in the midst of the family's grief, the Greek Orthodox priests refused to allow the body to be buried unless Shoulis recant his Protestant faith. Distressed by the loss of his child and scorned by his wife and mother-in-law, Shoulis, in desperation, denied his beliefs. The priests then performed the funeral with a full Orthodox liturgy, requiring Shoulis to actively participate in the many rituals. Afterwards he deeply regretted his actions and eventually asked to be restored again to the Protestant church.

This event served as a painful reminder to Gerasim of the many difficulties they had to overcome if they were to establish an Albanian-speaking Christian community in a place where the Greek Church wielded such power. He therefore began searching for a property to purchase where Protestants could bury their dead.[8]

Thomson now decided to reprint two versions of the Tosk Psalms, one in the former Greek alphabet and a second in the new letters. As Gerasim corrected the sheets, he became aware of a number of discrepancies between Kristoforidhi's Albanian translation and the English and Bulgarian texts. He mentioned this to Thomson who thought little of it at first, but then, to his dismay, realised Kristoforidhi had not translated the Psalms from the Hebrew texts as had been claimed, but from a much later Greek translation of the Hebrew called the Septuagint. The entire book would have to be revised. What had begun as a mere correction of the press now became a laborious and time-consuming affair. Gerasim rose early each morning and worked late into the night to find the extra hours required to carry out the work.

Since coming to Kortcha Gerasim had also encountered problems with the Austrian postal service. Foreign governments had operated such services in the Ottoman Empire since the eighteenth century. Letters or parcels were taken to an embassy or consulate from where they were collected and forwarded to their destination, often arriving within a few days. Gerasim's first four letters from Thomson had been suspiciously delayed by several weeks, and his letters to Istanbul arrived opened.[9] He was clearly once again under the watchful eye of the authorities.

During this time Gerasim and Athena received many visitors. People came to discuss various topics, from spiritual matters to the future of the national educational movement. Gerasim developed a close friendship with Petro Nini Luarasi, the new director at the Albanian school who had replaced Pandeli Sotiri, now in Istanbul. In Petro, Gerasim found a friend who shared his passion for the gospel and determination to see Albanian schools established. Another teacher from the school, Thanas Sina, was also deeply affected by Gerasim's preaching.

The Albanian boys' school in Kortcha had become the target of strong opposition. The Greeks and Turks, through their influence over the Muslim and Orthodox *millets*, threatened severe consequences against any family who dared send their children to the school. As a result, the number of pupils dropped sharply in 1890 and many who had previously donated funds dared not continue.[10] With dwindling financial resources, the trustees were unable to cover their expenses. Pandeli, in whose name the permission for the school had been issued, was unable to continue his work after going several months without pay.

Facing financial ruin, he left Albania and returned to Istanbul. The boys' school struggled on without him.

Other attempts to open Albanian schools in Erseka and Pogradec had not survived such persecution. Gerasim considered these problems as he planned for their girls' school. He knew it was imperative they secure an irade before beginning, but such a thing seemed impossible. Might Naim Frasheri help them secure one as he had done for the boys' school? What Gerasim did not know was that the mutasarrif had been told by the vali of Monastir: 'This school [the boys' school] was opened as it was opened, leave it ... but see to it that no others are started'.[11] Gerasim wrote asking Thomson to meet with Frasheri and seek his advice on how best to proceed.

The priests kept up their weekly denunciations, deriding Gerasim for failing to observe the traditions of the Orthodox Church and accusing him of reviling the holy saints and the sacred images. They also called him a *mason*, implying he was a member of an enigmatic and potentially seditious sect. Gerasim reassured the people his sole purpose was to present the Albanians with the word of God in their own tongue.

In all their labours, Gerasim and Athena worked under difficult circumstances with very limited financial resources. They grew tired and were prone to infections. Athena also became pregnant at this time, but suffered much with illness.

On 14 February 1891, Thomson sent Gerasim an encouraging letter:

> I have a little good news for you. Mr. Sellar reads of course
> your letters and knows all about your work & your pro-
> posed female school. He is the Superintendent of the

Bebek Sabbath School which collects a little money for
missionary purposes, one for the African Congo Mission
and the other has hitherto been for the Kurds. But as
we get little or no information about the work among
them, Mr. Sellar suggested that we should give half our
collection this year to the Albanian Mission, and he even
retained a part of last year's collection & sends it to you.[12]

It was their first pledge of support for the proposed new school.
Rev. Thomas Brown and the Turkish Missions Aid Society
would later add to this small but promising beginning.

Gerasim now applied to the authorities for official recognition of a Protestant community in Kortcha. As yet, however, too
few dared openly profess Protestant faith to satisfy the minimum
requirement under Turkish law. He therefore limited his request
to permission for a Protestant cemetery as a private person.

Gerasim's and Athena's mothers both came to Kortcha to assist in delivering Athena. On 30 March 1891, she gave birth to a
boy whom they named Stefan. Thomson wrote the proud father:

It is a new and a wonderfully stirring thing to feel the
new-born affections of a father for a child, with all its
anxieties and responsibilities. It gives a new impulse to
the heart, and a sense of dignity. And then it enables us
better to understand the tenderness and love of God to
us poor sinners, for He calls himself our Father in heaven
and encourages us to trust him, as we do earthly fathers.[13]

There was little respite amidst the joy. The vali of Monastir
now vigorously resisted colportage. Thomson applied for help
from the embassy only to find the ambassador 'luke-warm in

supporting our rights, both commercial and intimately connected with the far higher principles of liberty of conscience
and worship'.[14]

Baird, who had been ill for several months, visited Kortcha
in April 1891. During his convalescence he had studied Albanian
and was now quite fluent. With years of experience in dealing
with Ottoman officials, he advised Gerasim on how to obtain
a license for the school. They also discussed the possibility of
further American Board involvement in the Albanian mission.
Baird now considered moving to Albania, possibly Berat, but
the final decision lay in the hands of the American Board's
Prudential Committee in Boston.

In Shkodra, George continued to suffer with poor health.
The rheumatism in his feet had been aggravated by the damp
climate of the city 'so that he could neither sit, stand nor lie,
or do anything'. He also found living alone difficult, with
no family to keep him company. Thomson wanted to send
Shoulis and his wife from Monastir to Shkodra, but Shoulis
now thought of leaving the Bible Society and so was unsure.
Gerasim needed George to join him in Kortcha to help with
the growing work, but there was no money for this. They
would also have to find more funds if they were to open the
girls' school later that year.

And then, at the end of April 1891, Athena fell seriously ill.
It began with a cough that did not improve. Over the weeks as
Gerasim watched her health decline, his anxiety grew. He asked
leave to take her to Istanbul, where her parents now lived, and
where she could receive proper medical attention. While there,
he could also finish correcting the Psalms.

Thomson agreed, and in early June Gerasim packed their cases and prepared Athena and Stefan for the two-day carriage ride to Monastir, the first leg of their long and tiresome journey. She would never return.

From a postcard of Kortcha, early 1900s

CHAPTER 10

THE BEACON LIGHT

AS GERASIM AND HIS family made their way to the capital, Sevasti prepared for her graduation. She was very proud of her school, the prestigious American College for Girls in Constantinople, which had begun with just three pupils in a rented house in Istanbul in October 1871.

The following year, at the 1872 Annual Meeting of the American Board in Boston, a proposal was put forward for a 'high school for girls', and the Prudential Committee resolved that 'such a school is urgently needed in Constantinople'. The Women's Board of Missions was given the responsibility to undertake a fund-raising campaign. Soon the women of the American churches collected $58,000 in voluntary gifts and donations and on 13 August 1872, the American Board authorised the purchase of land in Scutari, near Istanbul. The founders had a clear vision:

> The design of the High School shall be to provide for the thorough education and Christian culture of girls from the surrounding various native communities, and for a special training of such as may desire to become

teachers and helpers in the missionary work... Pupils will
receive a thorough drill each in her own vernacular by
competent native teachers, instruction in the Bible, in
Arithmetic, Geography, Algebra, Geometry, Chemistry,
Botany, Physiology, Hygiene, Natural, Mental and Moral
Philosophy, Vocal Music, Needlework and Weaving. The
English language will be so thoroughly taught that it may
be made the medium of instruction in advance studies'.[1]

Physical geography, history and geology were later added to the
curriculum.

On 6 January 1876, the teachers and pupils moved into the
new building, which became known as 'The Home'. Over the
entrance were the words, 'This house for God'.

An annex was added in 1881 with a grant from the Prudential
Committee. The following year, William Chapin gave $20,000
from his personal funds to build Barton Hall in memory of his
late wife, Sarah Barton Chapin.

By 1889, dozens of girls from 12 nationalities had received
their educations from the college. On 18 February 1890, an
Act of Incorporation by the United States Senate and House
of Representatives gave the school, now called The American
College for Women in Constantinople, the right to function
with full legal standing as an American institution of higher
education.

The college had over seventy boarders during the years
Sevasti studied there. She gave it high praise:

As regards the College, as a whole, so firm and so sure
were its spiritual foundations, and so wise and loving its
building, that it could not fail to prosper. The home spirit

and the general feeling of friendliness was a real joy also to all the students. We were not only taught the value of a high standard of work, but also the benefit of outdoor play, gaining both health and pleasure from the one mile walk in the grounds every day and the croquet and tennis matches played in the garden. The garden parties were a delight to us all, not to mention the picnics at Chamledja, the beautiful mountain height behind Scutari. Beside there were interesting and instructive lectures of prominent visitors to Constantinople, which broadened our horizon.

The development of this great institution now occupying the beautiful buildings on the hilltop overlooking the Bosphorus, has been a big and difficult task — a work of many anxious years; a work of highest ideals and aspirations. The Faculty and Trustees deserve much credit and enjoy, certainly, the heart-felt gratitude of the alumnae, for being so faithful to their trust.

What I personally owe to the college cannot be measured, but I can say that there I got the wider prospect of life, living in an atmosphere of high purposes and of work for its own sake. I can never be grateful enough for what Constantinople College did for me.[2]

Her years in Istanbul were formative and the teachers modelled a style of education she would one day emulate in Albania. An excellent student, Sevasti was also tenacious and daring, traits that would serve her well in later years. In her memoirs, she recounted her 'first adventure', which occurred during her last year of college in Istanbul. It is a story that would have dismayed her parents and one which is well worth recounting here in its entirety.

For most of us the period of learning is a time of romance. I was young and ready to attempt even the impossible.

While at College, I heard from different sources that in the famous prison of Yedi-Kuleh, on the Bosphorus, there were many prominent Albanians, among whom was a certain man named Koto. The story of his heroic life made a big impression on my mind and gradually there grew in my heart a strong desire to have an interview with him. So I worked silently and cautiously, hoping finally to enlist the aid of the superintendent of the prison, Qamil Effendi, who happened to be an Albanian. I had luck. One day, quite unexpectedly, I found out where this Qamil Effendi and his family lived. The next day I went to see his wife and we soon became friends. She often invited me to spend the day with her. One noon during dinner, I turned the conversation to the subject which was so near to my heart and asked Qamil Effendi whether there were any Albanians in Yedi-Kuleh prison. He mentioned a few names and, to my delight, Koto was one. The assurance that he was still there stirred me more than ever, and I determined to leave no stone unturned until I saw this patriot of ours, who had bent all the force of his understanding and energy to helping his country.

One day I summoned up my courage, donned the garb of an Albanian boy, and went to visit my friend, the superintendent of Yedi-Kuleh. When I walked into his office, he was not a little surprised at my appearance and asked,

'What brings you here, my girl? Why have you run the risk of coming to this place disguised and alone? You have shown great courage; but listen, never venture to take another risk of this kind!'

'I see no risk I met with no unpleasant experience,' said I.

'Well, you had *kismet* [good luck].'

'Yes, indeed. I have confidence that my *kismet* will not fail me this time. With this confidence I have come to beg you grant me a favour of great importance to me.'

'Tell me what it is,' he said impatiently: 'and I will grant your wish if it is in my power; but please do not ask the impossible.'

'I just beg you to let me see Koto — a favour which I shall never forget.'

I took him by surprise, but after meditating for some time, the superintendent gave me the permission, though reluctantly. We walked to the gate and here he called for a man to guide me to Koto's cell. The guide took a lantern and a bunch of keys and we started to descend into a labyrinth which had never seen the light and did not deserve the name of 'habitation'. Only a few rays of light coming from the distant loopholes and the lantern of the guide helped me to see where to put my foot. The narrow, winding corridors that led to the dungeons were like a spider's web. The air was damp and foul, and chilled me to my very bones. Soon, we started to descend steep stairs. A feeling of great depression overwhelmed me. Another turn and some more steps led us down — to what depth, I dared not imagine! Here we came to a corridor where I suddenly was seized with terror. Groaning, sighing and cursing could be heard on all sides — an Inferno, more real than Dante's. At last we came to the end of this long corridor. Here I felt a continuous thudding against the walls. I opened my mouth for the first time and inquired of the guide what this strange noise was.

'Oh! It is the waves of the sea beating against the walls of the fortress,' said he. Then he pointed to a small door, which he opened. A terrible sight lay before me

as we entered, causing me to shudder. A filthy hole! A
streak of light from a loophole above helped me discern
a miserable figure, but I could not make out whether or
not it was human. On a slab of stone that served for a bed
it laid huddled in a heap of rags. Koto! My first impression, when I saw him, was that all his intellectual faculties
were extinct, and I asked myself, 'Is it possible that in this
miserable and frightful body lives the soul of Koto, the
great Albanian leader?' Oh, I have no power to describe
the miserable state in which this martyr dwelt.

'Tungjatjeta, Koto!' I finally dared to murmur.

'Who is it that is talking to me? It must be some heav-
enly voice sent by God to speak a soothing word to my
wounded heart,' said he in a feeble and hardly audible voice.

He raised himself with great effort, for he was half-
dead. My guide bent over, propped him up against the
stone wall, where he made a picture of such misery that
I felt hot tears rolling down my cheeks. Hair long and
beard matted reaching down to his waist, garments the
merest rags. I spoke almost choking.

'I have come, dear father, to bring you a word of encouragement and to tell you that though you have been
thrown into this dungeon to suffer cruel torment, still the
seed that you have sown is bearing good fruit, and your
spirit lives in the heart of your people.'

'Yes. They have chained my body, but my soul is free.
It is free, and no torture can prevent me from crying: 'No,
Albania will not perish. She will soon be united, independent and happy! But kindly tell me, dear daughter, who
are you and what made you risk coming to this miserable
place?'

'I am an Albanian student at Constantinople College
and during the last two years there I have heard a great

deal about your noble deeds. I came to beg you to tell me just what is the cause of your present misery, for I feel that your story will be an inspiration to me, as I have decided to devote my life to the enlightenment and uplift of my Albanian sisters.'

'You know Turkey was defeated in 1877?'

'Yes, I do.'

'Well, Turkey, after her defeat, ceded to the victor more than half of Albania. Certainly the Albanians could not tolerate this great injustice and rose up to defend their fatherland by force of the sword. Our movement was very successful, and Europe was compelled to retire and restore to Albania a great part which had treacherously been joined to its neighbors. Well, after three years, Turkey began to understand that this movement might finally lead to independence, and as soon as it was convenient, the Turkish Government made every effort to dissolve the League by violence and treachery. It was during this time that a great number of our compatriots were arrested, imprisoned and exiled; and I fear some found their graves in the depths of the Bosphorus. I am one of the victims of this policy of the Sultan.'

'But I have heard that the Sultan wanted to pardon you.'

'Yes, my daughter, but at the price of my giving him the names of the people who organized the Albanian League. How could I possibly betray the leaders of our first national movement? The Sultan, when I refused to comply with his request, said to me, "Koto, don't you know that your head is in my hands?", and I replied, "Yes, Majesty, I know it too well. My head is in your Majesty's hands; my soul belongs to God, but honor is mine!" It was this retort that brought me here.

I swallowed my tears and asked him, 'How is it, dear father, that after three years of successful struggle the League failed?'

'It failed because Turkey divided our people into Moslem and Christian, for the policy of the Sultan is *"divide et impera!"* We cannot possibly become an independent nation until we enlighten our people and help them to understand that, though we differ in religion, still we are all Albanians. Education is the weapon which kills tyranny, and I am glad that you have decided to devote your life to the enlightenment and uplift of your Albanian sisters. Undoubtedly you will meet what seem like insurmountable difficulties, but be brave like a true Albanian and you will overcome them. Inspire all those who come under your influence with high ideals and lead them to truth, which alone can make a nation great.'

Here we were interrupted by word from the superintendent to leave for it was getting late. As I bade Koto farewell, he said, 'You have brought me a ray of light to give me life, and strength to bear my burden.'

My heart was so full that I do not remember how I got out.[3]

Determined to begin her work for the national cause as soon as possible, Sevasti studied at an accelerated rate, finishing the normal four-year course in three.

On Friday, 26 June 1891, a special Commencement Day was held in honour of the graduating class. The week before, Sevasti and her six classmates had been taken to a beautiful garden on the Asiatic shore by the Sea of Marmora, where 'class literary speeches and merry-making were enjoyed'. A dinner was prepared for them, hosted by the faculty of the college.

On Commencement Day many friends and guests filled Barton Hall to participate in the celebrations. Among them was the renowned American missionary, Dr. Edwin Bliss, as well as representatives of the American Legation, the Bulgarian Exarch and the Patriarchs of the Armenian and Greek churches. But by far the greatest honour for Sevasti was the presence of the illustrious Frasheri brothers, Abdyl, Naim and Sami. Gerasim also attended, having arrived in Istanbul just two days before.

The hall was brightly decorated with flowers and flags. In the centre of the stage stood a basket 'containing the beautiful Diplomas which had been sent from Boston, tied with the College ribbon of blue'. Music was performed and songs sung, essays were recited in various languages, and the President of the college presented the diplomas.

Naim Frasheri, representing the Ministry of Education, addressed the assembly. Speaking in French he said: 'It is an established principle that the good education of the young is the cause of moral progress, and this Institution is considered by the Imperial Government to fulfil its role perfectly, and of this the fete of today gives fresh proof.'[4]

After the ceremony, Gerasim introduced Sevasti to the Frasheris. Naim said to her:

> Sister, you cannot do a better and more valuable work for Albania than what you have already decided to do with your brother for the emancipation of the women of our poor little country. If you are faithful and perseverant, you will accomplish great deeds for our nation.

He added the greatest wish of the Albanians for the fulfilment of any mission, — 'May you come out with a white face!' — that is, 'May there be no material or moral blemish to mar the nobility of your achievement'.[5]

Naim took her diploma for registration in the Ministry of Education. This was the first step in obtaining an irade for their school. The next day Sevasti said her final farewells, and began her journey back to Monastir.

Gerasim now had other concerns. At her parent's home in Istanbul, Athena grew ever weaker. As he continued his work on the Psalms, Gerasim anxiously watched and prayed for her recovery.

Back in Shkodra, George was restless. Shoulis had agreed to remain with the Bible Society and moved to Shkodra, but the thought of another winter in the cold, damp climate of that city was more than George could bear. The American Mission had offered him a salary of four lira a month to work for them but he declined, deeming it insufficient. George now wanted to visit Istanbul to discuss his situation with Gerasim, but Thomson would not agree to pay his fare. He wrote to George:

> If I saw any good that would be got in your coming here I would allow it, but I see none. The case is very plain. The funds of the Board are very low, so that they are lowering the salaries of their missionaries all over the world, and lessing their expenditure in every possible way. And hence they cannot offer you as much as they might otherwise do. But it is also to be taken into consideration that I gave you so large a salary because both Seefried and Thoshe said that the dearness of Shkodra was the cause of their getting into debt. And moreover also the American Board

does not give so high salaries as the Bible Society to its colporteurs, who are almost constantly travelling about. As a preacher you would not travel about so much. I would earnestly recommend you to accept the offer of the mission, for I have no hope whatever that any other society will enter on the Albanian work.[6]

When his contract with the BFBS ended in August 1891, George left Shkodra and sailed for Thessaloniki, unsure of his plans. There he met with the head of the American Bible Society in Thessaloniki, Mr. Bowen, who immediately offered him a position in his depot. Thomson, who had helped pay for George's education to prepare him for work in Albania, was angered by Bowen's proposal and wrote to George:

I consider you owe service to your own nation, both as a Christian patriot, and because you were educated for that very object. Think and pray over the matter.[7]

Concerned that he might be lost to the Albanian work, Thomson wrote to Bond in Monastir with a new proposal. If the American Board would give George four lira per month to work as a missionary in Kortcha, the Bible Society would pay another one and a half lira for him to do some colportage. Both Baird and Bond agreed, but their offer came too late. George had already accepted Bowen's offer and Bowen now refused to release him from his contract.

Back in Istanbul, Athena's condition was deteriorating. Thomson described the situation to Secretary Paull in London:

But I regret to say that Mrs. Kyrias is very weakly and her disease, pulmonary consumption, leaves little encouragement to her anxious husband.[8]

Gerasim worked on. He completed revising the Psalms in September and, at the beginning of October, bid an emotional farewell to his wife and son before boarding the train for Thessaloniki, from where he would continue to Monastir and Kortcha.

It was a time of both joy and sorrow. To Gerasim's amazement, Naim Frasheri had managed to secure an irade for the Albanian girls' school. What had seemed an impossible dream was about to become a reality, but his wife's illness weighed heavily on his mind and spirit. Baird received a letter from Gerasim at this time that he concluded 'in a rather sad tone, quoting an Albanian proverb: 'When the poor man began to dance the drum burst'.

Gerasim arrived at his parent's home in Monastir and met Sevasti. They had planned to leave for Kortcha in the second week of October, but George arrived from Thessaloniki, delaying their departure. They spent hours discussing the situation together, anxious to find a way for George to join the work. Sevasti prepared lesson plans for the school. One day a telegram arrived from Samokov offering her a position at the girls' school there, but her mind was made up, 'she was going to Kortcha and Samokov would have to look elsewhere'.[9]

In the end, George reluctantly returned to Thessaloniki and, on 20 October 1891, Gerasim and Sevasti boarded a carriage for Kortcha.[10]

As they travelled along, they spoke of many things. At Laithiza, Gerasim pointed out the place where, years before, Shahin and his band of brigands had descended into the valley and carried him off into captivity. Sevasti shuddered at the thought. Throughout the journey, Gerasim told of the numerous and difficult challenges which lay ahead, and explained how Albania's misery had been caused by misrule and incompetence. Sevasti would always remember his words:

> Yes, it is the oppression by the Turks which has brought about this period of stagnation in our country. Our people are industrious and diligent, but of what use are such virtues under the present régime? All our money is taken from us in taxes, and none of it put back into the country. We have practically no roads, and the lack of proper roads, as you know, hinders transportation and obstructs trade. As a natural consequence, poverty is everywhere, and, as we are forbidden to have our own schools, ignorance reigns. A number of our more enterprising young men, having emigrated to Egypt, Romania, Bulgaria, and other countries, and having by their labor and thrift accumulated some capital, have made generous gifts in reply to the cry for schools; but, unfortunately, these gifts have fallen into the hands of the Greek bishops, the leaders of the Christian communities, who are using them to hellenize our people instead of to educate and uplift them. You and I have all the greater responsibility, now that these other projects have failed. How our Albanian friends in the [Ministry of Education] ever succeeded in persuading the Sultan to grant us the permit to open the school is still a mystery to me. But so it is, and our great chance lies before us.[11]

Though overwhelmed by the challenges facing them, Sevasti was thrilled to at last be working with her brother. His confidence inspired her with courage. In her memoirs she recalled how even his enemies considered him a 'tower of strength'.[12] Nineteen years old and just out of college, Sevasti could hardly believe she was about to begin the task she had so long prepared for. As they approached the town she carefully observed every detail:

> We entered Kortcha from the north coming through Broad Street to the home of my dear brother, which stood side by side with the church of St. George, the Albanian patron saint. How excited I was when we reached the home where Gerasim had been living and where we were to start the school that I had been planning for so many years. It was a large and pretty house with six big rooms and two large halls, and, as it stood in the center of the city, I was able to see from my window a great deal of activity. The liveliness of the inhabitants and the cleanliness of the place were signs of prosperity…
>
> The population of Kortcha is almost entirely Albanian, with a very small minority of Vlachs. Also, at the time of my arrival, there were a few Turkish officials and officers, a few Greek teachers and of course the Greek bishop. The inhabitants were divided in religion: out of 23,243 inhabitants 17,779 were Christians belonging to the Eastern Orthodox Church and 5,464 were Moslems, and the Sublime Porte as well as the Patriarchate were doing their best to keep them divided. The schools helped greatly to this end.
>
> Besides the public schools, where only Turkish and Arabic were taught, the Patriarchate, on the basis of the privileges granted since 1453, had opened a number of

schools in Kortcha for the Christian population. In these schools the Greek language was taught and Greek history occupied two-thirds of the time, their purpose being to hellenize the youth of Albania and to claim Kortcha for Greece; but the Albanians would not be hellenized.

Kortcha was coveted by the Greeks for its rich natural resources and for its strategic geographical position. So, pushed by greed, they declared that Kortcha was Greek and did their best to present it as such to the outside world, with the hope of grafting it some time on to Greece, together with the rest of southern Albania. For this purpose, the bishop had organized the Christian community under the name of 'The Hellenic Community of Kortcha', and, under threats of boycott, excommunications and denouncement to the Turkish authorities as rebels against the Turkish Government, had succeeded in forming a strong pro-Greek party, forcing the people to send their children to the Greek schools. Side by side with this, there was in Kortcha a pro-Turkish party. Both parties, though hating each other, fought ferociously any attempt to emancipate the people from the yoke of these foreign propaganda. At the time I arrived in Kortcha, Greek propaganda was rife, and the very atmosphere breathed an air of threat against any attempt to have the people taught in their mother tongue. The bishop even went so far as to preach on Sundays, 'The Lord's command is that all Christians must study only the Greek tongue and must worship in Greek, for God does not understand Albanian and accepts no worship in the Albanian language.'[13]

Back in Monastir, Baird and the other missionaries were keen to support the Albanian work, but Baird's health was still poor and mission funds were lacking. Also, the vali of Monastir had begun to inquire more closely into the American Mission's activities in Monastir. In October 1891, Baird wrote to Secretary Clark in Boston:

> The government is looking after schools rather sharply. For the first time it has asked for the diplomas of the teachers and the course of study including the textbooks. These have been in the hands of the government here for two months but are not finally acted upon yet. It appears that everything has to go to Constantinople for approval.[14]

While Sevasti prepared one of the rooms in the house as a classroom, Gerasim again visited the families of Kortcha, inviting them to send their daughters to his sister's new school. The Greek party followed after him, threatening the severest consequences for anyone who dared to enrol their children there.

Fear of reprisal from the leaders of the Greek Orthodox Church caused most families to keep their daughters at home. When Sevasti opened the doors for the first day of school on 23 October 1891, just two days after their arrival in Kortcha, only three girls came.

It was an overwhelming challenge. Sevasti found them ill-prepared for studies and even basic discipline was a problem. In her annual report at the end of the first year, she said:

> We knew from the beginning that the burden we had taken upon ourselves was heavy and the task difficult, for much patience is required and great endurance, but the feelings we have for our nation make us forget all the obstacles and opposition which may arise, and make

us weary in this work. The burden is heavy because the
girls with whom we are dealing have never been taught
any lessons in their homes, they have not learned to obey
proper orders, nor have they been given any spiritual
education from their parents, but we are comforted by
the word of the song which says: 'Perhaps with tears
and sorrow you sow the seed, but be patient. For a day is
coming after these troubles, when you will reap with joy
and happiness'.[15]

Reflecting her own experiences at the school in Monastir and
the American College for Women in Istanbul, Sevasti developed
this threefold programme for teaching the girls:

I. Firstly, it is physical exercise to maintain good health,
for without good physical health, knowledge is of no value, and does little good.

II. Secondly, it is mental exercise, to have good and sound
judgment and to gain that knowledge which is necessary
for everyday life.

III. Thirdly and most valuable for the girls is spiritual exercise. A sound and enlightened spirit is extremely valuable
for them to understand. If they are taught to work properly and to befriend God's law, they will do every task well
and will never be ashamed in their work. The fear of God
and the knowledge of His law, is the first duty of man and
we can say all things beneficial to man depend on this.[16]

To many it seemed an insignificant beginning, but for Gerasim
and Sevasti it was a day of small things not to be despised.
Though numbers were low, eventually more and more families

dared to defy the Greek party and began sending their daughters to the school. Despite the rumours and slander spoken
against them, brother and sister enjoyed much support from
the townspeople, including several of the Muslim beys.

And thus, against incredible odds and in the midst of many
enemies, the 'Beacon Light', as the school came to be known,
was lit. But then, in December 1891, the telegram Gerasim had
dreaded arrived from Istanbul. Athena's end was near.[17]

Sevasti Kyrias (photo courtesy of Niko Kotherja)

CHAPTER 11

DEEDS OF DARKNESS

ALEXANDER THOMSON'S LETTER OF 28 December 1891 to
Mr. Bosdoyannes, the superintendent of colportage at Yanina,
closed with news of Athena's death:

> You will be sorry to hear that Mrs. Kyrias, daughter of
> Rev. Stavros Michaelides and well-known in Yanina, died
> December 24th and was buried on the 25th. She was full
> of faith, hope and peace, and her last hours were a living
> and a most impressive sermon. Mr. Kyrias is here at pres-
> ent. He has an infant son.[1]

Gerasim's 'dance' had been short lived indeed. He grieved,
but there was little time for grief. Too young to join his father
in Kortcha, Stefan was left in the care of Athena's parents in
Istanbul. But as Gerasim was about to depart on 9 January, his
fever returned and he was confined to bed.

Meanwhile, the Ministry of Education continued to refuse permission for the Bible Society to print the Psalms that
Gerasim had so painstakingly revised. Naim Frasheri, claiming
to favour the request, told Thomson it had been opposed by

the Minister on 'pretense of agitation among the Albanians'.[2]
Thomson brought the matter before the embassy and the
ambassador met with the Minister who, to his surprise, was ig-
norant of the entire proceeding. Thomson wrote concerning
the ambassador's meeting:

> On talking with the Minister of Instruction, he said he
> had never refused the permission and knew nothing at
> all about it. In short, it was found that it was Naim Bey
> himself that alone opposed us. When I called, he advised
> me to print it with an old permit, which should have
> involved a falsehood, and that I said I could not do. He
> then found fault with the orthography in Greek letters,
> and though I told him that we were to publish another
> edition in the new letters, he still resists us. We shall see
> whether he or the British ambassador will prevail.[3]

Frasheri opposed the Bible Society on this issue, convinced
that one alphabet alone — that of his brother, Sami, and the
Istanbul Committee — was best for the nation. There had been
sharp disagreement between Kristoforidhi and the Istanbul
Committee on this point, but Thomson's primary concern was
for the scores of Tosk Albanians who only knew Greek letters
to be able read their publications. For the moment he intended
to continue with two alphabets. Nonetheless, Pandeli Sotiri had
already begun revising a transcription of the Psalms into the
new letters, which they planned to print in Bucharest.[4]

Gerasim intervened and met with Frasheri. Encouraged by
their discussions, he reassured Thomson of Frasheri's intentions, saying he was 'an intelligent and reasonable & just man,
desirous to give us our rights & to promote education among

all classes of the people'.[5] Nevertheless, Frasheri remained
opposed to Thomson's request.

In January a new British ambassador, Francis Clare Ford,
replaced William White, who had died suddenly while visiting
London for medical treatment. One of Ford's first official duties
was to discuss the problem of the Tosk Psalms with the Sublime
Porte. He was told the matter was to go before the Sultan. Relieved at this, Thomson wrote: 'So we now know where it is,
and if it is rejected, we shall know that it is the work of the
Sultan himself'.[6]

For now, the printing of the revised Tosk Psalms would have
to wait.

While in Istanbul, Gerasim also visited his friend Pandeli
Sotiri. Together they discussed Gerasim's idea to start a new
Albanian periodical using the irade issued in Pandeli's name
with which the Albanian Committee of Istanbul had previously
published the Dituria. Pandeli consented and agreed to serve as
editor.[7]

A new Albanian colporteur now worked the streets of
Istanbul. Thanas Sina, former teacher and one-time director
of the Albanian boys' school in Kortcha, had been introduced
to Thomson by Pandeli Sotiri in November 1891. Sina, a 'quiet
and intelligent man', became one of the Bible Society's most
faithful employees and would later revise all of Kristoforidhi's
translations. Sina's New Testament revision was republished by
the Albanian Orthodox Church after the fall of communism in
Albania, for use in their liturgy.

When he sailed for Thessaloniki at the end of January, Gerasim was still unwell. There he met his brother, George, who had
grown weary of working with Bowen and now expressed a very

strong desire to move to Kortcha. Arriving in Monastir, Gerasim reported this to the missionaries. Baird wrote to Bowen with a request that George be released for ministry in Albania but instead, Bowen increased George's salary and demanded he finish his contract. George's frustration with foreigners was growing.

Together with Baird, Gerasim returned to Kortcha on 5 February 1892, pleased to find that, despite growing persecution, Sevasti had done well in his absence. There were now thirteen girls in the school and a large number of women attended her Bible classes, learning to read as they studied the scriptures.[8]

Baird stayed in Kortcha for several weeks and was very impressed by the work. Moved by Gerasim's ability to carry on despite the death of his wife less than two months before, he wrote:

I am surprised at the consolation he receives from on High and at his laboring personally with individuals, in season and out of season to bring them to Christ. Tho' his wife's sickness & Dr. Thomson's work have taken him away a good deal from this city the work does not seem to have gone back. He is pressing hard and persistently to secure, 1st, a place (by purchase) for preaching and a girls' school. These both are in his own hired house from which he expects to move next August. It is very hard to get a place by renting for these. 2nd for a periodical in Albanian, say semi-monthly. Not one of any kind exists at present. Two influential men of the place, one a Moslem & one Non-Moslem called to talk on this subject. The latter, one of the leading merchants of the place, offered to take and pay for in advance, if necessary, 200 copies for this region. There is no doubt that such a periodical will, if issued, be a great blessing. The greatest obstacle in the road is the laws and customs & irregularities of the government. The next is the money question as I can hardly believe that there will be sufficient subscribers to pay the expenses.[9]

Gerasim now turned his attention to fund-raising. Their success thus far had been the result of tremendous personal sacrifice and dogged determination. They took no fees from the girls in the school. Personal gifts from Thomson and donations from the Turkish Missions Aid Society and the Sunday School in Bebek had enabled them to carry on, but they now needed buildings and furniture, books and supplies, and trained pastors and leaders. And all these cost money.

In March 1892, Gerasim and Sevasti wrote a detailed letter describing their plans for the school, the church and the periodical.[10] It was read at the Annual Meeting of the European Turkey Mission in Samokov in April and sent to Boston for the consideration of the American Board's Prudential Committee. Greatly encouraged by these developments, the missionaries responded by designating 145 lira for Albanian work for 1892–3.[11]

Back in Monastir, the vali now seemed determined to put an end to the Bible Society's activities in Macedonia. He issued an order requiring the colporteurs to present lists with the names of all the towns they planned to visit on each tour for his personal approval. This special 'service' was charged an additional tax that quickly increased from three piasters to ten and then 20 per request. A time-consuming and costly affair, the men were thus prevented from selling outside the city for months. Concerned that such measures might become standard procedure in other districts, Thomson again appealed to the British ambassador.

Gerasim dealt with such problems whenever he visited Monastir, but Baird was often called upon to intervene on behalf of the Bible Society. This loss of time from 'endless excuses of the officials for perpetual delays' led Baird, who now planned to settle in Kortcha, to suggest that Gerasim move back to Monastir to deal with the Turkish authorities himself.[12] At this stage, however, Gerasim was intent upon remaining in Kortcha.

Another threat to the work arose in 1892 when the Sublime Porte required the registration of all buildings used for educational or religious purposes. This decree effectively enabled the government to prohibit schools and churches from operating by denying them use of buildings for such purposes, even though an irade had been granted for the activity itself. Several foreign powers condemned this as a violation of the treaties the Ottomans had enacted. The British Prime Minister, Lord Salisbury, instructed his ambassador in Istanbul 'to oppose any such restrictions on the liberty of conscience & freedom of worship'.[13] In April 1892, the British Embassy together with the American Legation told the Porte they would not permit the closure of any school which had been opened by any missionary, 'even if it was held in his house', without satisfactory cause.[14] This came as encouraging news to Gerasim who still awaited final permission for their school from the vali of Monastir. He hoped they too would enjoy American and British support in the matter.

At the same time, Gerasim's concern was growing over the potential implications of increased American Board involvement in their work. Would the American missionaries cooperate with them, or simply try to take over what they had so painstakingly begun? He wrote to Thomson on this matter who reassured him his 'position as the Bible Society Sub-Agent and as a native Albanian preacher or Pastor will always enable you to maintain your views with dignity'. Nevertheless, George in particular remained wary. Thomson wrote:

> No doubt there are disadvantages with foreigners, and with the best intentions they may and will make mistakes. But I confess I see no way of our prosecuting the mission without their taking it up, as the Churches in America may be able and willing. I have neither the time nor the power to raise funds for the work, and I confess I cannot understand how George expects to work for his people, unless he consent to work in harmony with the American Mission. It is a very serious question, and I hope you will think over the matter very seriously yourself and try to persuade your brother to modify his views. He would not have to work under the missionaries, but would be taken into counsel with them, which is very different.[15]

Their need for finances was a determining factor. On 23 April 1892, Pandeli Sotiri visited Bible House in Istanbul. While waiting for news of the intended periodical, Pandeli, now virtually penniless, had transcribed several New Testament books into the new letters hoping to sell them to Thomson. But as the Bible Society's annual expenditure had exceeded its income by £24,000, the Committee in London issued an order for all its agents to 'practice the utmost possible economy'.[16] Thomson could not buy the manuscripts.

But now, with the grant of 145 Turkish lira from the American Mission, they could at last hire Pandeli and start publishing the periodical. Gerasim sent a letter to Thomson for Pandeli with the good news. Thomson was much relieved to receive it at the beginning of May, for he had heard a disturbing rumour:

> I earnestly hope that Mr. Baird and you will arrange to get the *Dituria* started soon, both because I think it will be an admirable thing for the Albanian people, and because it will, I hope, give some occupation to Pandeli Sotiri. He seems to be in great distress, and Eliah told me today that he had heard from somebody, an Albanian, that he was seriously ill, if not actually dead. He was here on Saturday the 7th, and told me of his distress, but seemed quite well. Eliah has taken your letter to him to Makrinkany, a village 5 miles from this city. I hope he will bring me good news, for I like Pandeli.

Tragically, Gerasim's letter had come too late. Thomson received the terrible news on 14 May 1892:

> Poor Pandeli Sotiri is dead. Your letter to him came just after he had left me, & I never saw him again. I now return all that was in the envelope. You may perhaps hear full accounts from Thanas Sina, or others; all that I know is this. After I had told him that the Society could not at present direct the Albanian [New Testament] to be copied into the new letters, because our funds are very low, and because we have still a large stock of the old Albanian books on hand, and because before copying it out in the new letters, or in the course of doing so, it would be desirable also to have the translation itself revised by the best Albanian scholars we have. So I was sorry to have to say I could not pay him for such work. But while he told me

he was suffering with his wife & children, I had no idea he was in such absolute want. I gave him twice half a lira; but had I known, I would have given him more; for I loved him and respected him very much. The next thing I heard of him was on Wednesday last, when Eliah told me that Pandeli had fallen, or it was feared had thrown himself, from a window in Pera and had died some hours afterwards. Oh, I cannot tell you how sad I was on hearing such news. How little I had imagined that he was on the brink of despair. It seems he had a rich acquaintance or relative, a flesher, in Pera, but after he identified himself with the Albanian party, that man would not help him.[17]

Gerasim was deeply shocked by the death of his friend. And with him had perished the irade with which they intended to publish the periodical.

Meanwhile, in response to pressure from British vice-consul Shipley, the vali of Monastir had 'withdrawn all claims upon the colporteurs of the British and Foreign Bible Society for any money payment beyond the ten piasters chargeable for their annual license as booksellers'.[18] But this concession did not denote any change of heart on the part of the vali. Despite an earlier promise to 'withdraw his aggression against the colporteurs of the British and Foreign Bible Society and the American Societies', the vali had simply found new ways to frustrate them. And so would he continue.[19]

Such unrelenting opposition was discouraging both to Gerasim and the other workers. Jovancho's sales were low and Thomson told Gerasim he needed to be 'stirred up to greater zeal & diligence'.

And so too with all of the men, and with ourselves too, my
dear Sir. We all need to be baptized anew with the Holy
Spirit in order to serve the Lord with new zeal & love.[20]

In June, the girls' school celebrated the end of its first year with
a public examination of the pupils, including a fete, speeches,
dramatic presentations and special music, all in Albanian and
all written by Gerasim. Sevasti stood before a delighted crowd
and gave her report for the year. Their enemies looked on in
indignation, furious their efforts to close the school had failed
thus far.

New premises were needed for the school and church. Gerasim continued looking for a suitable property, but their lack of
finances was a great burden to him.

Then, in July 1892, there was further bad news. Thomson
received an order from London to reduce colportage expenses
by at least seven or eight hundred pounds by the end of the year.
All colporteurs with poor sales records were to be dismissed. In
Shkodra, Shoulis had done little for months and was informed
his services would be terminated at the end of August. In Skopje,
Jovancho too faced dismissal. Gerasim went to visit him in July.
The two men travelled together to Prishtina. During the journey
Gerasim saw that Jovancho's problems had resulted neither from
indolence nor carelessness, but from the difficult nature of his
territory and the aggressive policies of the vali of Kosova. With
Gerasim's intervention, Jovancho was allowed to keep his job.

Afterwards Gerasim visited Thessaloniki. George, having
made the most of his time there, was about to marry Myrine
Athena, the daughter of a colporteur named Zaphirius, a 'good
man', with many years service to the Bible Society. Gerasim

probably attended the ceremony, which was performed by Dr. Mihailis Kalopothakes of Athens in July.[21]

George pleaded with Gerasim to help him find a way to join the work in Kortcha. His contract with Bowen had finally come to an end and the American Board was now offering him a salary of three liras a month to assist Gerasim, but he feared he could not support himself and his wife with so little. Gerasim could suggest no alternative. George wrote to Thomson offering his services, part-time, to the Bible Society for an additional one and a half lira a month, but Thomson was still under strict orders to economise and so could not oblige.

Back in Monastir, Gerasim met with Fanka Efthimi and Gregor Tsilka. Fanka had now finished her course at the girls' school in Samokov and, with support from the Turkish Missions Aid Society, would join Sevasti teaching in the school. Gregor had also accepted a position with the American Board to work in Kortcha. In August 1892, Gerasim, Gregor and Fanka boarded a carriage for Kortcha accompanied by Lewis and Fanny Bond. As they travelled they discussed the prospects of the work before them.

Gerasim had been able to collect funds for a chapel and schoolhouse from sources in America, as well as from the missionaries, from friends in Bucharest and others. Upon his return to Kortcha, he bought a plot of land and, as soon as the title deed was signed over, hired builders to begin the work.

This purchase infuriated the bishop of Kortcha who unleashed a fresh wave of hostility against Gerasim. The acquisition of property threatened to give the Albanian work permanence, a development the bishop adamantly opposed. Threats, accusations and slander had accomplished nothing.

The school was still operating and Gerasim was more highly regarded than ever. As the foundations were being laid for the new building the bishop decided the time had come for more drastic action.

In early October he drafted *anathemas*, or ecclesiastical curses, against Gerasim and his associates for 'disseminating anti-Christian teachings and forbidden books' that aimed to 'corrupt our holy faith'. These were read publicly in the churches, and also printed and distributed widely throughout Kortcha and all Kolonia.

The following anathema against Petro Nini Luarasi was written in Kortcha on 2 October 1892. Translated by vice-consul Shipley and sent to consul-general Blunt in Thessaloniki, it was signed Philaretos, 'Your Well Wisher', and reveals the depth of Greek vehemence toward the Albanians and the Albanian cause:

> To the most reverend clergy, notables and all other Christians blessed in the Lord dwelling in the villages of the Eparchy of Kolonia entrusted to us by divine providence greeting: Grace to you and peace from the Lord and from ourselves prayer benediction and pardon.
>
> With great grief we have seen and heard during our recent visitation in the above district that the accursed and excommunicated Peter Luarasi has, in connection with the Protestant and Masonic propaganda, been visiting various villages of the Colonial district promising to appoint Albanian professors ostensibly for the teaching of Albanian, a language which does not exist, but in reality that he may pervert the consciences of the adherents of the Orthodox religion and gain converts to Free Masonry and to Protestantism. Moreover we

have learned that the above deserter and traitor to our
Orthodox religion has promised thirty Napoleons at
one place, twenty five at another, and twenty at another,
for the purpose alone that he may shake the foundation
of our Orthodox faith which our holy martyrs, fathers
and teachers have strengthened by so many sacrifices
and by their own blood. We say that this is his only aim
viz.: to corrupt our holy faith since these Free Masons
and Protestants have already begun to revile the holy images, to dishonour the noble cross, to abolish fasts and
to scatter abroad New Testaments and emissaries and
other books which are contrary to our holy religion and
which our mother the great church of Christ has already
years before excommunicated and burnt. On account of
these things therefore we, being moved by our paternal
solicitude, exhort all of you small and great, poor and
rich, men and women to put no faith in the words and
promises of these accursed renegades, to shut your ears
to their blasphemies and to remain all of you faithful to
the religion of our fathers which we have now held for
eighteen hundred and ninety two years; otherwise; we
announce and declare in our Episcopal right and by nature of the divine Spirit which our Lord Jesus Christ has
bestowed upon us through his holy disciples and apostles
that whosoever shall receive money from the accursed
Peter Luarasi and his fellows or that accept an Albanian
teacher or Mason or Protestant books, is excommunicated of Almighty God and receives the curse of the
three hundred and eighteen and remaining fathers of the
Church, shall be afflicted with the leprosy of Gehaz, and
his body shall remain undissolved and reviled after death
neither shall any good or profit befall him in this world

until having repented he shall have obtained canonical
pardon and absolution.

> Philaretos in Christ of Kastoria,
> Your well wisher.[22]

Reaction against the anathemas spread quickly throughout
the Albanian communities at home and abroad. The President
of the Albanian Committee of Bucharest, Nikolla Naço,
sent a protest to the Minister of Justice at the Sublime Porte
threatening to take legal action against the bishop to 'make
the Patriarchate refrain from politics & respect the Albanian
nation'. Naço continued, 'The Patriarchate by its organs called
holy has just daringly cursed our language, & practically denied
our existence'. For Naço, their purpose was clear:

> The intention of the Patriarchate is to separate the
> Albanian Christians from the rest of the Ottoman Empire
> and attach them to the Kingdom of Greece.[23]

Gerasim's concern was growing that the Greeks might resort
to violence against them. Since returning to Kortcha in August,
he had been aware of an increasingly sinister element in the
bishop's opposition. Thomson tried to play down his fears and
wrote,

> The enmity & opposition of the clergy will do you no
> harm, if of all poor, guilty, perishing sinners.[24]

But only days after the anathemas were published, Gerasim's
neighbours began to notice three men repeatedly prowling about
his house at night-fall, enquiring where Mr. Kyrias's bedroom

was, and other particulars, which plainly indicated that they contemplated burglary and violence and most probably murder'.[25]

Sevasti recalled part of the incident:

> One morning… at dawn, my attention was attracted by an armed stranger walking up and down under the window of the house facing the street. I was suspicious, but said nothing to my brother. The next day our landlady saw him and called my attention to him. Both mornings, my brother had gone out to the school building before the appearance of the suspected man. At noon when my brother returned, I informed him, but he did not take the matter seriously, and dropped the subject. I did not drop it. The next morning, before brother left the house, I went out and inspected the street round our premises before letting him go. I watched until he had turned the corner of the street, when lo and behold, the strange man appeared nearby. When he saw me standing in front of the gate, he withdrew immediately. The next morning the landlady asked him what his business was prowling round her house. He made no answer but disappeared.[26]

Gerasim eventually called for a zaptieh and the men, who he described as 'lawless and well-known', were arrested. Soon after they were released without charge. Someone of influence had clearly intervened on their behalf.

News of the incident caused Gerasim's popularity to soar. He was fast becoming a local hero whose courage inspired others to take a stand for their nation. Many townspeople who had previously remained aloof now came to discuss matters of a spiritual nature. Attendance at the church meetings increased significantly. His enemies, however, were simply biding their time. They would soon strike again.

Gerasim, Sevasti, Gregor, and Fanka supported each other in the face of such adversity. Sevasti spent 'most of her time among the women visiting and conducting prayer-meetings in which she [met] with much to encourage her', while Fanka concentrated entirely on teaching in the school. Gregor Tsilka worked among the men of Kortcha, finding 'favourable opportunities for religious conversation, especially in the market'.[27] Gerasim carried on his duties with the Bible Society and visited families, which the Greek clergy had tried to intimidate. Anyone who attended the Albanian service or sent their girls to the Albanian school was publicly rebuked by the church officers and faced the 'loss of all services of priests for baptisms, funerals and other religious ceremonies if the offence was repeated'.[28]

The fear of having no place to bury loved ones kept many families from allowing their girls to attend the school. Gerasim had purchased a piece of land for this purpose, but just as his request for permission was about to be approved, the Greek party intervened and succeeded in delaying the proceedings.

Gerasim continued to struggle with limited funds. On 14 October 1892, he wrote an appeal to the Mission in Samokov, which was later published in the Missionary News, a periodical of the American Mission. He describes their joy over the new school property:

> I am sure this purchase is in answer to our prayers. For the last three evenings this has been the subject of our prayers. Happily we had not hired any house up to the

present. There will be room for a family to live in the building. We may have some difficulty in the beginning because we don't have all the money needed, but I consider it a great step forward in the Lord's work here. My sister likes the location. It is a healthy place and has a nice view...

...Your interest in the work among our people has done a great deal of spiritual good among our brethren here. They feel greatly indebted to the church in Samokov, and we are glad to notice the spirit of gratitude in them. Now they understand better how not only individuals but whole nations can be bound in the love of Jesus Christ. Now they understand better that giving is preaching.

We are very happy in securing such a building at quite a small cost, which meets all our present expectations. The hall, used for school and meetings, is 9 by 5 metres, and holds over 100 hearers. In the same story is a room in which one of the teachers lives. Downstairs are two rooms occupied by the family of a colporteur who pays five liras ($22) a year, with which income we will meet the school expenses.

The cost of the building, including all expenses for repair &c. did not exceed 165 Turkish liras. Our debt today is 27 liras, an insignificant sum compared with our prospects, and we hope to get rid of this debt before the beginning the new year. You know that we have tried to secure a place for a cemetery and at one time thought the question was settled, as the money was paid, but some hindrances were put in the way and the matter was referred to Constantinople. We insisted upon having the place and very often bothered the governor about it. At last, yesterday, it was finally settled that we should have the place. Now there is room provided both for the living and the dead. The securing of these two places should be considered a good foundation, and a great step ahead in the Lord's work among this people; but our most earnest desire is to secure living stones for building up a nation which will be called the Lord's.

The officials are aware of the plot against my life which was recently discovered, and one day, while we were discussing the cemetery question in the government, they were somewhat amused at my remark, 'If anything happens we ought to have secured the grave-yard lest the confusion shall be greater when the Greeks refuse to allow us room in their grave-yard.'

You have probably heard that during the last three months the elders of the Greek church and the clergy have been very busy in their vain efforts against the Lord's work, using all possible means to injure it. We paid little attention to what they spoke against us, because we had a more important work to do. We can never bark as they do, and it would be a foolish work to undertake fighting with such people. Our indifference and steadily doing our duty has discouraged them, and it seems that the storm is over, the means of persecution being all exhausted. They had prepared some rules according to which no religious rite would be performed in the houses of those who attended our meetings or send their daughters to our school. These rules were not approved by the Patriarch at Constantinople and, as soon as this was known here, the girls in our school began to increase in number. They asked also their religious head to allow them to read the gospel in Albanian in their church, so that they may prevent people from attending our meetings, but they did not get a favourable answer.

We expect my brother and his wife early next month. Both have shown great love for the work, and I hope they will be useful here. When they join in this work I shall be able to make tours, to visit our brethren in different parts of Albania and, if possible, to open work in other places. I shall need, before long, to go to Bucharest for publishing work. My hands are full of work. Special grace has supported me in such a variety of duties, with a wide correspondence in several languages, superintending colporteurs in Albania and Macedonia, accounts, building, services on Sunday and prayer-meetings, unexpected business, etc. I am exceedingly glad that my brother is coming here.[29]

CHAPTER 12

THE
'EVANGELICAL
BROTHERHOOD'

IN THE COURSE OF a year, Gerasim had lost his wife, Athena, and his friend, Pandeli. The Greek Orthodox Church had publicly cursed both him and his associates, and an attempt had been made on his life, the assailants being released by the courts. With his son, Stefan, in the safety of Athena's parent's home in Istanbul, Gerasim, much like a sheep among wolves, now resolved to withstand the violence of his enemies and remain in Kortcha.

Early in November 1892, George and his wife arrived in Kortcha, accompanied by Baird. Tired of waiting for further support, George had accepted the American Board's 'very small salary' of three and a half lira to serve as assistant missionary to his brother.[1] They moved in with Gerasim and Sevasti. To make ends meet they would have to live most frugally, but for George it did not matter. He was, at long last, working in Kortcha.

Such was the impact of their Albanian worship service at this time that Kortcha's Greek Orthodox Church began to include Albanian readings in its liturgy.[2] Before long, however, the Patriarch of Constantinople forbade the practice.[3]

As he was overseeing the construction work on the school and church building, Gerasim turned his thoughts to the other towns and villages of Albania. How could they be reached? What more could be done? And then he had an idea.

As mentioned above, various societies had been established to promote national education and the development of Albanian literature, but these were all based abroad. Gerasim decided to create a national society inside the country. The girls' school was making good progress and Petro Nini had established five new schools in his home district of Kolonia. They had many friends across the nation and beyond. With clearly stated goals and objectives, such a society could rally broad support and encourage new works in other places.

On Monday, 14 November 1892, Gerasim called the founding meeting of the society in Kortcha. Among those present were his brother, George, and sister, Sevasti, Gregor Tsilka, Herakli Bogadini, V. Pasko of Pogradec, Fanka Efthimi, and most likely Petro Nini Luarasi. They gathered to draft a constitution, choose a name for the society and elect officers. Their discussions were long and lively.[4]

They agreed upon an eight-article constitution, which gave the aims and rules of the society. Shipley translated part of it in a report to Blunt in Thessaloniki. Articles one and six were as follows:

ARTICLE I

A fraternity of Evangelicals has been formed here in Kortcha, which has for its sole object the propagation of the Gospel and the development of Albanian literature in Albania by every lawful method.

ARTICLE VI

It is the duty of the Committee to carefully superintend all matters concerning the school, to determine the times of meeting of the assembly and to decide generally what is to be done; further to present their report as to what has been done with regard to the schools, as well as upon any wants the latter may have. They shall have the supervision of the teachers and mistresses and together with the latter shall draw up the school program. The Committee shall also undertake the duty of seeing to the publication of books.[5]

They called their society the *Vëllazëria Ungjillore*, or 'Evangelical Brotherhood'. They probably chose the term 'evangelical', rather than 'Protestant', to best describe the nature of their work. Their mission was based on the *ungjill*, or gospel, while the word 'brotherhood' defined their purpose — to unite the people to work for the good of the nation. The society's seal would include three symbols; a quill pen, a bottle of ink, and an open book.

Ten names were written into the member's roll that night, with 'more expected'.[6] Gerasim was elected president, and George treasurer.[7]

John Baird, who also attended the founding meeting of the Evangelical Brotherhood, was aware of Greek hostility and reported to Secretary Clark in Boston: 'There is some opposition especially from the ecclesiastics and as the Albanians are a little more under the control of priests than the Bulgarians are, the opposition has kept away & still keeps many away from the services — especially the women...'[8] Gerasim had expected nothing less and told Thomson ruefully, 'the Greek clergy will never help the Albanians... They wish to frighten the people'.[9] Nevertheless, Gerasim now considered Albania 'the most hopeful mission field of the Balkan Peninsula'.[10]

Another decision of the society was to begin publishing a new periodical, a bold step considering the anathemas and possible assassination attempt. It was to be called *Letra e Vëllazërisë* [The Letter of the Brotherhood], and would declare the aims of the new society and inform the nation of their progress. The first edition, printed in Kortcha in November 1892, on a hectograph donated from Samokov, was the first attempt to publish an Albanian language periodical inside Albania.

Written by Gerasim and courageously published with his name and address, this first 'Letter' exuded a spirit of confidence and hope, and called the Albanian people to action. It opened with a clear statement of the society's purpose, to develop the Albanian language and spread the gospel, and continued by lamenting the fact that so few Albanians knew the beauty of the gospel teachings. 'If they are of such value,' asked Gerasim, 'why should they not be read in Albanian in the Albanian churches?'

> If the Albanians desire to see their country civilized, prosperous, and contented, a knowledge of these teachings is imperative for it is through them that a feeling of true

fellowship is created, sincerity and truth promoted and the various evils which exist among us removed.

Gerasim compared the stagnation into which Albania was plunged with the clear progress visible elsewhere. 'Even the savages of Africa understand that without knowledge their lot cannot be bettered'. He warned the Albanians not to deceive themselves:

> The immediate necessity of the nation is for paper and pens and a knowledge of its own tongue without which it is impossible to advance on the right path.

He reminded parents of their solemn responsibility to see their children educated and to learn their duty toward God and their country in their own language. 'The disgrace will indeed be great of remaining in darkness when the light is shining all around'.

Gerasim invited his readers to respond after giving the matter their careful consideration. He included a brief report of the seven Albanian schools that had already been opened and explained that permission for the girls' school in Kortcha had now been granted by the authorities in Monastir.

Gerasim concluded with a stirring appeal to his fellow Albanians to unite in the task of spreading light in their own country, assuring them 'no aim can be nobler': 'The Albanians have worked sufficiently for others; it is now time they should work for themselves'.

Through distribution of the 'Letter,' news of the Brotherhood spread quickly, reaching even diplomatic circles. British vice-consul Shipley in Monastir sent a translated summary of it to Blunt in Thessaloniki, including it in a report in which he anticipated problems for the new society.[11]

Blunt met with leading Greeks and Albanians in Thessaloniki to learn more of the nature of the new movement. He concluded that the Turkish provincial authorities were simply following 'the same astute policy of non-interference which they have always pursued in dealing with the national and religious rivalries between the different Christian races under their rule', adding, 'as the movement seems to be favoured and assisted by Mahomedan Albanian Beys, it may also be countenanced by the Turkish Authorities so long as it does not degenerate into a factious political agitation'.[12]

Blunt forwarded Shipley's report together with his own observations to the ambassador in Istanbul and included a translation of the anathema (Fulmination) of bishop Philaretos. He explained:

The Greeks, whose sentiments are expressed in the enclosed Fulmination of their Archbishop, are alarmed, not so much for the danger to their church, as by attempts of a rival race, which they have always considered and represented as being entirely under Hellenic influence, to maintain its language and assert its nationality.

The same feeling animates them in the futile resistance which they still offer to the national movement of the Bulgarians and Vlachs in Macedonia and is doing incalculable mischief to their cause. The more enlightened Greeks at Thessaloniki look with unfeigned alarm at the existing state of affairs in this province and disapprove the actions of their clergy in resisting the developments of the vernacular used by the different races professing the Orthodox faith. They consider that the growing desire of these races for the use of their own language in churches and schools is perfectly legitimate...'[13]

With the establishment of the Evangelical Brotherhood and publication of the 'Letter', Greek efforts to eradicate the work intensified. Gerasim soon grew 'much annoyed by the conduct of local authorities under the influence of Greek clergy'.[14] Once again he asked Thomson to apply to the British Embassy for help in securing their rights.

Work on the church and school building neared completion. As they prepared to lay the foundations for a new room, Gerasim gathered materials to place inside a memorial capsule. They held a special ceremony and sealed it into the cornerstone.[15]

Many encouraging letters came in response to the 'Letter of the Brotherhood'. A second edition was published in December, but the quality of the hectograph was poor so they did not make many copies. Nikola Naço, president of the Bucharest Committee, offered to print subsequent editions in Bucharest free of charge and also asked to officially join the Evangelical Brotherhood.[16]

Baird now arrived with a proposal for George to start a new work in Berat, which surprised both George and Gerasim. There was already more than enough to do in Kortcha and dividing their efforts would render them less effective. Gerasim approached Baird to discuss the matter, but he seemed determined to follow through with his plan.

There were windows and doors to build, public worship meetings to conduct, Bible studies to prepare, classes to teach and more. They used the hectograph to print a hymnal with twenty-four hymns and held special meetings for singing. A younger brother came from Monastir in December and helped George build a bookcase for the new school library.[17]

In early January 1893, a special week of prayer was held for the work. On 13 January, the Evangelical Brotherhood met to discuss three subjects: the problem of drinking, member's duties, and the need for Albanian schools.[18] Each Sunday over seventy people, as many as could fit inside, attended the Albanian service in the new chapel.

Gerasim continued to use the Magic Lantern to great effect. He enchanted large crowds with the beautiful pictures and the stories he told. One day he visited Alo Bey at his home and impressed him with this marvel of modern technology.[19]

And then, as the work was reaching its most promising state, Gerasim's enemies made a second attempt on his life.[20] On 17 January 1893, an armed man described as 'a murderer', entered his house, 'evidently intending to kill somebody'.[21] Outside, a young accomplice kept watch on the road. Gerasim went for help and George led the man into the yard. In a drunken state, he 'uttered words clearly revealing his intentions'. Unable to locate a zaptieh, Gerasim returned, but finding them still there, he left again. When he came back the second time he was accompanied by an officer who arrested the men and threw them in jail.

Sevasti's memoirs include an account of this event, but with some variation in detail. The discrepancies can be explained by the fact she wrote from memory more than 40 years later:

> ...the servant girl announced that a certain man wished
> to see Mr. Kyrias. Going down, I found that the stranger

had darted into our house and had already entered our dining room like a butcher unto a slaughter pen. A troubled look knit my features for he was armed to his teeth. I wished to do a little fighting in my own way and get rid of this treacherous man. So I greeted him and asked him to be seated, but he refused and acted queerly. A loud shout burst from my mouth. I was unable to conceal the deep anxiety I felt, and I was very impatient to hear from his treacherous lips some statement regarding his errand.

'What is your errand, man?' I asked him.

'I shall deal with Mr. Kyrias. This is no business for you. You'd better hurry up and tell him to come right down!'

At the same time I heard footsteps and turning round saw my brother coming down. Like a flash I ran and said to him, 'Don't come down! A murderer is waiting for you. Your blood is worth more in your own veins than anywhere else. I will not consent to your risking a drop of it.'

He smiled and said, 'Be quiet, dear sister! No harm will come. Let me see who it is and what he wishes.'

And so brother quietly came down and entered the dining room. He shook hands with the stranger, spoke kindly and asked what his errand was, expressing at the same time his readiness to help him if he was in need of anything. A courage worthy of the soul of a hero! When the to-be assassin was drawing his revolver to shoot, the spirit of my brother brought a change to his wild shifting eyes and his revolver dropped in his pocket and said, 'Mr. Kyrias, do you know why I am here? I was to ask you to write a letter for me and then while you were stooping, to stab you; but I cannot do it now that I have met you. God forbid that I should stain my hands with your innocent blood!'[22]

Convinced of the bishop of Kortcha's complicity in the scheme, Gerasim suspected he was acting on 'higher orders from [the] Patriarch or from Athens'.[23] Though Gerasim considered the men's punishment necessary, he desired that the real perpetrators, those who had put them up to it, be exposed, and thus prevent such acts from recurring. He asked Thomson if the British Embassy might appeal to the Sublime Porte to send orders to Kortcha to have the affair investigated 'more diligently'.[24] Such an investigation would prove that his enemies opposed him simply because 'he preaches the gospel to the people in their own language'.[25] Without such orders, Gerasim feared the local authorities would allow themselves 'to be bribed or give way to pleadings'.[26] In early February, Thomson asked the British ambassador to intervene on Gerasim's behalf:

May I therefore earnestly support the petition of Rev. Mr. Kyrias, that your Excellency would represent this matter to the proper authorities, and procure the transmission of stringent orders to the local authorities of Kortcha & Monastir, to have this matter thoroughly investigated, and every precaution taken against the repetition of such criminal proceedings.

I may add that Mr. Kyrias knows well the character of his own nation, for which he is labouring so earnestly: for seven years ago he was seized by Shahin, a noted robber, and his band, kept in captivity for six months with cruel treatment, and only liberated at last by the payment of a high ransom by the Bible Society.

Soliciting your Excellency's favourable attention to this affair I have only further to say that the Patriarchate and the Greek Church all over Greece and Albania have resisted the preaching of the gospel to the Albanians in their own language, and the circulation of the Albanian Scriptures, entirely, as it would seem, because the use of their own language would frustrate the plans of the Greeks for Hellenizing them, incorporating them among the Greek nation, and claiming the whole of Albania ultimately as Greek territory. A strange perversion this of the office of the Church of the living God, to make it an engine of political ambition & aggrandizement, in utter neglect of the commands of our Lord to preach the gospel to every creature … in the language he understands.[27]

As they awaited the trial, several immediate and positive effects from the incident became apparent. The accused was a known criminal and 'all Kortcha seems to be glad that this man has been imprisoned, a brigand & murderer'.[28] Many could now 'see better the wickedness of the Greek clergy & understand better the truth of the gospel'. As a result, Gerasim perceived a 'wide door' of opportunity and enjoyed even greater support than before. Numbers attending the Sunday services rose sharply and there was renewed interest in spiritual matters. Encouraged that 'many souls were coming to Jesus Christ',[29] he was aware that people no longer called him 'a mason'.[30]

The trial, held in mid-February, did not last long. When it was over, the young accomplice went free and the brigand, who had admitted his guilt and against whom witnesses had testified, was sentenced to just three months in prison. Though it was the second attempt on Gerasim's life in three months, no mention was made of a possible conspiracy. For Gerasim the verdict was clear. The authorities would not protect him from his enemies.

This time he was afraid.

CHAPTER 13

CLOSING EXERCISES

WITH MOUNTING PRESSURES, THE threat of assassination, the unrelenting opposition of the vali of Monastir and the Greek clergy, the responsibility of securing financial support for his co-workers and for the school, his work with the Evangelical Brotherhood as well as numerous other duties, it is extraordinary to think that Gerasim found the time or the equanimity to engage in creative writing, but write he did. During the early months of 1893 he prepared sketches, poems and songs for use in the school and completed a narrative of his six months as a prisoner of Shahin Matraku.

He tried to make his account of the capture both 'interesting and spiritual', to attract sympathy to 'these poor brigands' who, in his opinion, were 'not the only people to be blamed for this state of things'.[1] Over several evenings he read the story aloud to a fascinated audience. The event proved so popular that he was asked to repeat it in a larger hall. The original Albanian manuscript has unfortunately been lost but a translation of the English version of *Captured by Brigands* was published in Albanian in 1993 and again in 2016.

Much of the material Gerasim wrote for the school was collected and published in the book, *Hristomaci*, edited and published in Sofia by George eight years after his brother's death. At times light-hearted, or moving and inspirational, his works encouraged the children to incorporate virtues such as honesty, generosity, diligence, patience, and kindness into their everyday lives. Much of his inspiration was taken directly from scripture and translated into recognizable scenes from Albanian life.

Gerasim also used writing to express his faith. His poem, 'The First Day of May', extols the beauty of God's creation and includes a reference to Darwin's theory of evolution. It is ironic to think that in a future atheist state of Albania, May Day, the Day of the Worker, would take on a very different meaning:

> The first day of May, what freshness and beauty,
> The hills and the meadows in splendour arrayed!
> On the first of the month I too ventured forth,
> In the midst of such beauty a stranger!
> Wherever I turned fresh wonders I saw,
> From the hand of the Lord, who had made them.
> Bright birds flitted from tree to tree,
> And filled the air with the sound of their song.
> In truth, they were praising the Lord of the heavens,
> Hon'ring their Creator with all their hearts.
> But what first should I see as I entered the wood?
> What thought came to mind, in the midst of such beauty?
> — That this whole earth, blessed by the Lord,
> Was indeed made by him to bring light to our minds!
> Further on, a crystal stream welled up from the earth,
> It made your heart sing as it flowed on its way;
> Watering the flowers and every green thing,
> Even to look brought peace to one's soul.

In truth, as my eye took in all this beauty,
The living Lord's glory was what was revealed.
The world and its wonders, ordered by God,
Are a feast for the wise, delighting their eyes.
With all kinds of good things we have been blessed;
We bear his resemblance, with honour we're crowned.
But we — so wretched and weak, how soon we forget:
The God who's in heaven, he alone is our king!
Our mind full of darkness, how often we say:
'The world and its beauty are empty and vain'!
A thought so base and so utterly futile,
Comes only from those without brain or sense.
Heaven and earth should always remind us
Of the God who's above, we're dear to his heart!
How wretched the faithless, of their own selves unsure,
They look to the apes for the start of man's life!
Their only thought, woe for self and others,
Unaware, the wretches, how terrible their end.
O God who is truth, may we keep this in mind:
What we owe to you; let's not waste our time!
With all our hearts let's pay heed to your words,
For the answer to our problems look to you alone.
To seek your loving face every day of our lives:
If we would reign in life, there's nothing more dear.
Love, friendship — these have their source in God,
Those who find such treasures are so truly blessed.
How happy the wise, who understand life's aim;
Always on their heart: the other person's gain.
With joy and with gladness such folk will be crowned,
Their hearts of simple purity with the Lord's entwined.
But from my theme I've not wandered,
The first of May I've pondered:
All these thoughts, from this day have sprung.

Lord, may Albania's sons and daughters all
Be held, heart and soul, in wisdom's thrall![2]

One day, during the Muslim holy month of Ramadan, Sevasti
answered the door of the courtyard. There stood four tall, well-
armed men and she froze before them unable to speak. One
said to her: 'Miss, do not fear us, for now we are good friends of
Kyrias. Please tell us whether he is at home.'

Afraid it might be yet another attempt on his life, she refused to let them in. Gerasim, meanwhile, had entered the yard.
When they saw him, they 'expressed their joy like children'. As
they embraced, Sevasti looked on in disbelief. Gerasim showed
them into the sitting room where they were soon engaged in
lively conversation. After sunset, Gerasim ordered a meal to
be served, 'for these friends were the brigands who had captured him, and now they were to break their Ramazan fast with
Kyrias, their former prisoner'. The brigands had since been par-
doned by the government and now came to offer their services.
Before they left that evening, they swore to protect Gerasim and
the school and gave their *besa*, or word of honour.[3]

Convinced Albania was a 'chosen field', Gerasim found
much to encourage him. He was glad of the 'earnest zeal' of his
friend, Petro Nini, who wanted to return to Kolonia to be near
his family and 'open a place to preach the gospel'.[4] If only they
had more funds they could employ other workers and 'send
the gospel all over Albania'.[5] As it was, despite limited financial
resources and the actions of the Greek clergy, their success in
Kortcha had been considerable.

Opposition to the work continued. In March 1893, attempts
by the vali of Monastir and the local authorities to restrict

colportage were so frequent that Gerasim felt compelled to move back to Monastir from where, with the aid of vice-consul Shipley, he hoped to deal with the problems as they arose. Despite assurances from the Grand Vizier that orders had been sent to the vali of Monastir not to interfere with the colporteurs, both Marmaroff and Jovancho faced constant harassment. In an attempt to resolve these difficulties, Gerasim visited Monastir in April.

The thought of moving from Kortcha gave much cause for regret. A wholly Albanian town, Gerasim had many friends there and the local authorities were 'very favourable to Mr. Kyrias & have never given him any annoyance'.[6] The Albanian worship service was well attended and Sevasti and Fanka would miss his protection and encouragement. Gerasim hoped that George and the promising young Tsilka would remain to carry on some of his responsibilities.

Thomson appealed to the Committee in London to allow George one and a half lira a month for work done on behalf of the Society. He argued his case convincingly and, despite the 'straightened circumstances' of the BFBS, the request was approved. This additional income would help George remain in Kortcha.

At this time Thomson began a thorough review of all his accounts from 1888 to 1893. To his surprise he found that Gerasim was in debt to the Society. The problem had arisen when various expenses, such as Gerasim's trip to Istanbul when Athena was dying and moneys given to Sevasti while she was at college, were thought by Gerasim to have been paid for by the Bible Society. Without his knowledge, these had instead been charged to his personal account. The debt was now large and would take years to repay. Gerasim was stunned.

It was a heavy blow and possibly more than he could bear. There were no corners to cut, no lira unaccounted for in his monthly salary. The Turkish Missions Aid Society gave a gift of £20 to help, but Gerasim could not see his way to repay the rest.

Now the Greek clergy in Kortcha directed another wave of persecution against the school and church. As a result, ten of the forty pupils were withdrawn by their families.

In a desperate bid to stop his work, in May 1893 the Greek leaders signed a petition accusing Gerasim of sedition and demanding his expulsion from the city. Any person found guilty of this crime faced exile or possible execution. The Patriarch of Istanbul personally presented the document to the Sublime Porte from where inquiries were made to the vali of Monastir. The vali looked to Kortcha for further information regarding Gerasim.

Vice-consul Shipley spoke with the vali of Monastir, expressing his 'utter disbelief' at the charge which he viewed as 'groundless' and little more than a blatant attempt by Gerasim's enemies to be rid of him. The vali assured Shipley there was no reason for concern, for the government would not declare Gerasim seditious 'unless he were so'.[7] The investigation continued.

At the girls' school, the end of their second year approached and preparations were underway for the closing ceremonies. The children studied their lessons and memorised Gerasim's dramatic sketches, poems and songs. Together with their teachers, Sevasti and Fanka, they decorated the school hall with coloured paper and flowers and displayed the crafts they had made during the year. With an air of anticipation and excitement, 'Exercise Day' finally arrived.

The celebrations were scheduled to begin at seven p.m. on 27 June 1893, but by 5:30 p.m., the hall was already full. When three Ottoman officials arrived at seven o'clock, there were no seats left and they remained standing for the entire programme. Four hundred people crowded the room.

A four-year-old girl opened with a hymn and then the youngest girls recited a children's creed and sang a chorus. The older girls followed, enacting short dramas, singing songs and reciting poetry. Several women wept as they listened to Gerasim's moving and poignant poem, 'The Drunkard's Home'. The children were then examined in different subjects and Sevasti presented her annual report.

Though unwell, Gerasim attended the ceremony. Watching the presentations and seeing the progress the girls had made must have given him a deep sense of satisfaction as he recalled the years of struggle and sacrifice which had made it all possible. The day ended with many congratulations and words of encouragement.

But then, two days later, tragedy struck. Kortcha was rocked by a series of earthquakes, which destroyed many buildings and terrorised the population. From fear of being crushed by falling stones, people abandoned their houses to sleep in makeshift shelters in their courtyards or out in the open fields.

Gerasim too, in his weakened condition, slept in a shelter outdoors, but soon caught a chill in the cold night air. Alarmed by his rapidly deteriorating health, Sevasti and George decided to take him to Monastir.

This time he would never return.

Kenketore

Hymna
per nde
Faletoret te Ungjiorevet.

"Dyke kuvenduare nder vetehet tuaj
Psafma e hymna e Kenke opirteriote,
dyke kenduare dyke psafure Zotit
nde zemeret tuaj Efesian. 5:17.

Mimrografisure nde Korçe, 1893.

The hymnal Gerasim used in his worship services: "Song Book. Hymns for the worship houses of Evangelicals. 'Speaking to yourselves in psalms and hymns and spiritual songs, singing and making melody in your heart to the Lord' (Eph. 5:17). Mimeographed in Kortcha, 1893."

CHAPTER 14

'LAMTUMIRË' (FAREWELL)

IN THE FIRST WEEK of July 1893, Gerasim, Sevasti, Fanka, George and his wife, then heavily pregnant, arrived in Monastir. Their families were dismayed to find them suffering the effects of exhaustion and exposure. Gerasim's health was completely broken so they hired a doctor to care for him. Too weak to do any work, he was confined to bed for weeks.

Perhaps unaware of his failing health, Gerasim had been labouring intensively since April. Taking little rest, every free moment had been spent writing new material for the children at the school. Now as he lay racked with fever and fits of coughing, problems of work and finance perplexed and agitated his mind. How could he repay his debt? Where could he find more financial support for the mission? What more could be done to secure the rights of the colporteurs?

On 20 July he tried to take a walk, but soon returned to his bed. Suffering much discomfort, he contemplated leaving the heat and pollution of Monastir and visiting the mountains, but his doctor, offering little encouragement, dissuaded him.

There was more bad news to come. The Prudential
Committee in Boston had decided to reduce expenditure in two
fields, Armenia and Albania. It was another devastating blow.
George and Tsilka had struggled to live on their present salaries
and Fanka needed an increase over the twenty lira per year she
received from the Turkish Mission Aid Society. When George's
wife had complications while giving birth to their daughter,
Victoria, and the doctors demanded three and a half lira for
their services, Baird refused to give anything either for the un-
authorised trip to Monastir or for the emergency medical fees.
Though Gerasim eventually persuaded Baird to cover George's
travel costs, he feared for the future of the work. It would have
been better had the American Board never offered its help in the
first place, rather than starting something it could not finish.

With the impending cuts in the American Mission's expenditure for Albania, both George and Tsilka began to consider
other alternatives. George asked Bowen of the American Bible
Society in Thessaloniki to allow him to return to his former
post, but he refused. Tsilka desired to continue his theological
studies and so travelled to Istanbul to meet Thomson, seeking
advice as to where he might go. Though 'impressed with the
young man', Thomson, surprised by his visit, was unable to
help. Tsilka returned to Monastir.

On 14 August, his strength returning, Gerasim went with
Sevasti to Ternova, his birthplace, in the foothills outside
Monastir. After just four days in the fresh mountain air with
clean water and peaceful surroundings, his health and spirits
greatly improved.

Gerasim wrote to Thomson with a new proposal. With just
ten Turkish lira they could build an additional room on the

school property to use as the Bible Society's depot, thus saving money on rent. Thomson approved the plan and Gerasim sent word to George, now back in Kortcha, to begin building.

The girls of the school had missed Fanka and Sevasti and, while they were gone, continued meeting together each Friday to pray, sing and read the Bible. There was much excitement on 19 September 1893, when Sevasti, Fanka, and George's wife and infant daughter all returned to Kortcha 'in fine weather'.

Gerasim's health seemed to improve. His first doctor, whom the family suspected of foul play in his treatment of Gerasim, had been dismissed. Now, under the care of two new physicians, they began to hope for a full recovery, but it was not to be. His disease, pulmonary tuberculosis, was about to enter its final stages.

Gerasim continued his attempt to obtain an irade for the cemetery. The authorities in both Kortcha and Monastir had approved his request but the papers were 'lost' when sent to Istanbul for final sanction. Determined to succeed, Gerasim instructed Thanas Sina to ask Naim Frasheri to intervene on their behalf.

At the end of September, Marmaroff once again became a target for the local authorities. Despite having complied with every requirement, he was arrested in Kastoria, fined three lira 'on the ground that he had no license permitting him to sell books', and forced to return to Monastir. Denouncing these actions as 'intolerable', Gerasim arranged a meeting with the vali for 28 September. When Gerasim arrived at the vali's office that day, he was told the vali was unwell. The meeting was postponed.

Two days later, on 30 September 1893, Gerasim fell 'dangerously ill'. The symptoms of tuberculosis often progress slowly for many years, fluctuating with the sufferer's natural resistance. Now they would have all been present: loss of appetite, fever, night sweats, fatigue, and coughing up blood.

Fearing he would not survive the winter in Monastir, it was decided to send him to a more temperate climate. Thomson suggested Cairo but Gerasim's doctors felt either Athens or Corfu were suitable, both offering milder conditions and fresh sea air. Thomson wrote to Dr. Kalopothakes in Athens, asking him to arrange Gerasim's accommodation. But before he could attempt the journey, Gerasim's health would have to improve.

News arrived from Istanbul that permission for the cemetery would soon be granted. Knowing the cemetery was of vital importance to the future of the work, Gerasim was greatly relieved.

At the end of October, Gerasim's doctors declared him fit enough to travel, but an outbreak of cholera in Thessaloniki resulted in quarantine restrictions at the port. Unwilling to risk the several extra days in quarantine, Gerasim decided to brave the more demanding overland journey. In a letter dated 7 November 1893, he told Thomson he was about to leave for Athens with his younger brother, Christos. But as they prepared to depart, the weather turned cold and wet. Knowing another chill would prove fatal, the trip was delayed yet again. It would be for the last time.

During the final weeks of his life, Gerasim wrote regularly to Sevasti, offering support and encouragement as she and Fanka continued the work without him.

In December his left lung ceased to function and his right lung was seriously affected. Gerasim knew the end was near.

He wrote to Thomson, thanking him 'for the fellowship they had enjoyed together in the work of the Lord'. He also called for Sevasti to come from Kortcha. Brother and sister spent many hours together, Gerasim giving final advice and direction.

One day as she sat at his bedside, he handed her a notebook and said:

Sister, I did not wish to burden you with problems of a political character, but since my hour is approaching, I have decided to give you this little note-book. In it I have put down the main principles underlying the policy of the Sultan and the Phanar [Patriarch]. When you have the time, read it, for it will help you to understand why things change so unexpectedly here. In it you will find also some suggestions as to how to deal with the Phanariotes and the Turkish officials, who will never leave you in peace. I am sure you will always be faithful to your duty.[1]

Sevasti vowed to carry on the work of the school whatever the cost to which Gerasim replied: 'Now I depart in peace.'[2]

On 2 January 1894, he died at his parents' home 'in great bodily weakness, and utter failure of nature, but in great peace and comfort, resting on the precious promises of God in Christ Jesus'. He was thirty-five years old.

Though Thomson had expected the news, it came upon him 'with the power of a shock... that made me feel for the moment helpless'.[3] Weeks would pass before he fully recovered.

'This great loss', wrote Kristo Dako, 'was felt not only by the leaders of our nation, but also by all the people, for one of their greatest leaders had fallen. The members of the Greek clergy, enemies though they were, could not but admit his greatness and there was one thing which relieved them, that now there was no such man in Albania to succeed him'.[4] British vice-consul,

Howard Shipley, said of Gerasim: 'He was a profound, independent thinker and one of those rare souls who become immortal
because of their deep love and devoted service'.[5]

John Baird, who had first taught Gerasim at the station class
in Monastir years before, paid him the following tribute:

> Mr. Kyrias was a born leader, a tireless worker, an attrac-
> tive and impressive preacher, and a spiritually minded
> man. Where is the man or men who will take up the work
> from which the Lord has called this pioneer evangelist?[6]

As the family prepared his body for burial, they discovered a
paper hidden in the bedclothes on which Gerasim had written
his final poem entitled, *Lamtumirë*, or 'Farewell'.

> O land of my birth, I cannot endure,
> My heart is breaking over you.
> For very soon I shall leave your shores,
> And never more set eyes on you.
>
> O land of my birth, your children
> Are fleeing, forced to depart.
> Yet you will live, for ever more
> To grieve those dear to your heart.
>
> O land of my birth, how I've yearned
> My whole life long for you!
> Yet today cold earth will cover me,
> And I'll never more set eyes on you.

My Lord, why not leave me here longer,
To ease the yearning of my heart?
Then bring to my brothers' mind, Lord,
To serve you, and to play their part.[7]

Gerasim's yearning may have been 'covered in earth', but others would carry on the work he had begun and his vision for Albania.

Though she deeply mourned the loss of her brother, Sevasti returned to Kortcha, determined their sacred task would not fail. So too their brother, George, Gregor Tsilka, Thanas Sina, Petro Nini Luarasi, and others continued to preach the gospel, establish schools and promote the national cause. In the course of their lives, each would make a significant contribution to the development of Albania.

Many difficult challenges lay ahead. The path before them was filled with fierce and, at times, deadly opposition. But none of them would ever forget the one who had shown them the way. Gerasim's example of faith, endurance, passion and hope inspired them to persevere through many trials and press on toward the ultimate prize.

Workers of the Kortcha mission station, ca. 1894, after the death of Gerasim Kyrias. *Standing (left to right)*: Gregor Tsilka, John Tsiku, Thanas Sina, Luke Tira. *Seated*: Fanka Eftimova, George Kyrias, Sevasti Kyrias.

EPILOGUE

GEORGE KYRIAS REPLACED GERASIM as Superintendent
of Colportage for Albania and Macedonia, first in Kortcha
and then Monastir. Gregor Tsilka eventually secured a passage
to America and completed his theological studies at Union
Theological Seminary in New York. He returned to Albania
with his young wife, Katarina, in 1900.

Sevasti and Fanka faithfully carried on the work of the
girls' school. Upon graduation from the American College for
Women in Istanbul in 1904, Sevasti's younger sister, Paraskevi,
directed the school while Sevasti received further training
at Oberlin College in Ohio. The Bebek Sunday School, the
Turkish Missions Aid Society and the Women's Mission Board
in America continued for many years to fund the work of the
girls' school in Kortcha.

In 1896, Alexander Thomson retired as Head Agent for the
Bible Society in Turkey, his post taken by the Rev. T. R. Hodgson.
Until his death on 15 January 1899, Thomson directed his
attention to Albania and the Albanian people in whom he had
taken a special interest for nearly 40 years, giving generously
out of his private funds. He left a small legacy for the work in
Albania.

As the Albanians persevered in their struggle for national independence, the whole of the Balkans experienced conflict and strife, war and insurrection. In 1903 Macedonia became the scene of a bloody uprising with thousands of civilian casualties. Missionaries established hospitals for the sick and wounded and organised relief aid for the destitute. During this time, Sevasti met the English adventurer, anthropologist and author, Edith Durham. The two became fast friends.

The Protestant mission continued in Kortcha, first under the direction of George Kyrias, and later with the assistance of Gregor Tsilka and others. In 1908 the first foreign Protestant missionaries, Phineas and Violet Kennedy, moved to Kortcha under the auspices of the European Turkey Mission. Kennedy was a graduate of Princeton University and his wife, Violet, was the daughter of American missionary Lewis Bond and had grown up with Sevasti in Monastir. Another American couple, the C. Telford Ericksons, soon joined them. With Petro Nini Luarasi, Nuçi Naçi and Sami Bey as teachers, the missionaries opened a school for boys in Kortcha.

Soon afterwards Erickson moved to Tirana, and later Elbasan and Kavaya. Erickson eventually founded the renowned Agricultural Institute at Golem, overlooking the shores of the Adriatic near Kavaya.

In Kortcha, Gregor Tsilka served as pastor of the Protestant church. An ardent patriot and supporter of the Albanian cause, Tsilka was a friend of the Albanian guerrilla fighter and historian, Mihal Grameno. Grameno wrote of him:

In Kortcha we stayed in the home of Tsilka. Tsilka was the heart and soul of the national movement, a great and

brave man, unwavering though they had imprisoned him
for this reason, and he was educated. The services of this
patriot have no equal and no reward. Tsilka merits many
pages of our national history, inasmuch as he has been, is
and will die a patriot.[1]

On 14 November 1908, a special congress was held in Monastir
to decide which alphabet to use for the Albanian language.
Lasting seven days, it attracted delegates from all over Albania.
Speeches were made, papers presented and an eleven-man work-
ing committee elected to draft a final proposal. Both George
Kyrias and Gregor Tsilka served on this committee, with George
as secretary. 'The occasion was great', wrote Kristo Dako, 'for it
was the first Albanian congress of the kind ever held. Learned
Albanians, representing all classes of people, *Moslems, Catholics,
Orthodox* and *Protestants*, came together like brothers'.[2]

In 1910 there was a setback for the national movement
when the Turkish authorities, with one exception, closed all
Albanian language schools. Claiming American immunity,
Phineas Kennedy refused to obey the decree. For a time, under
American protection, the girls' school in Kortcha was the only
Albanian language school operating in the country. It was at
this time the school became known as *Shkolla amerikane*, or the
'American School'.

The British and Foreign Bible Society now began a revision of their Albanian translations of the New Testament, the
Psalms and several Old Testament books. Thanas Sina, who had
been introduced to Alexander Thomson by Pandeli Sotiri years
before, carried out the work.

Gerasim's close friend and associate, Petro Nini Luarasi, died in 1911, widely believed to have been poisoned by his enemies.

That same year, the American millionaire, Charles R. Crane of Chicago, who served as President of the Board of Trustees of the American College for Girls at Constantinople, visited Kristo Dako in Monastir. Dako had returned to Albania in 1909, having graduated from the University of Bucharest and Oberlin College. He married Sevasti Kyrias in 1910. Crane and Dako toured the country, visiting Ohrid, Elbasan, Tirana and Shkodra. As a result, Crane became an ardent financial supporter of the Albanian cause.

With the fall of Turkey in Europe in 1912, Albania at last gained her independence. On 28 November 1912, in the port city of Vlora, the Albanian statesman, Ismail Bey Qemali, raised the Albanian flag for the first time in nearly five hundred years. Many had given their lives for this moment.

For the better part of a century, the British and Foreign Bible Society had laboured among the Albanian peoples, publishing and distributing Albanian books and literature. In his evaluation of the Bible Society's contribution to Albania, the writer and patriot, Midhat Bey Frasheri, under his pseudonym, Lumo Skendo, wrote:

Above all I feel constrained to offer a just tribute of gratitude to the British and Foreign Bible Society for the services which it has rendered to our country and literature by its translation of the Holy Scriptures into the Albanian language. It is, in fact, impossible to speak of the language and literature of Albania without recalling the labours and the devotion of those who for so long, and in the face of so many difficulties, have carried on this noble work.[3]

George Kyrias died of heart failure on 30 December 1912. Shortly afterwards his wife and two children emigrated to Canada. Five years later in Sofia, while escorting his own daughter to the American College for Women in Istanbul, Gregor Tsilka's life ended during an outbreak of influenza.

In 1922, having spent nearly ten years in the United States, Kristo and Sevasti Dako returned to Albania and moved the girls' school from Kortcha to Tirana. Paraskevi also joined them there and, together with the financial assistance of Charles Crane, they established the influential Kyrias (Qiriazi) Institute, which was eventually located in Kamëza, a few miles outside Tirana. Today many of these buildings make up the agricultural institute there. The Kyrias Institute was a source of education for all girls regardless of social or religious background. Kristo, Sevasti, and Paraskevi each received the Order of Skanderbeg during their lifetimes, the highest civilian honour, but their school was closed in 1933 under a decree of King Zog, forbidding all private education in Albania.

At a congress held in Berat on 12 September 1922, the Orthodox Church of Albania severed its ties with the Greek Orthodox patriarchate. Albanian would now be the main language of the Church, not Greek. The patriarch of Constantinople, however, did not recognise the Albanian Orthodox Church as autocephalous until 1937.

Also in 1922, John Tsiku, Gerasim's faithful colporteur and friend who went on to serve many years with the Bible Society, died and was buried in Monastir in the same cemetery as Gerasim.

Gerasim's son, Stefan, orphaned before he turned three, was raised by Athena's family in Istanbul and Izmir. After graduating from middle school in 1908, Stefan was sent to Oberlin college in Ohio. He later studied engineering. In 1918 he married Hallie Gay Thomas, and they had five children together. Stefan lived in the United States until his death in 1959.

In 1932 American missionary Edwin Jacques together with his wife, Dorothy, arrived in Albania to assist Kennedy in the work in Kortcha. In 1933, the Kennedys' boys' school was also closed by Zog's decree and the mission restricted to religious activities only. The Kennedys returned to the United States in 1936, handing responsibility for the mission over to Jacques. Under Jacques' direction, the Protestant church of Kortcha grew to over 100 adult members and conducted an extensive children's work.

The outbreak of the Second World War and subsequent Italian occupation of Albania resulted in the evacuation of all foreign nationals. Expelled in 1940, Jacques was one of the last foreigners to leave the country. The work of the Protestant church in Kortcha continued, eventually in secret, under Albanian leadership throughout the war and into the communist period. Only a handful of these believers lived to see the restoration of religious freedom in Albania in 1991.

Sevasti and Paraskevi continued to live on the school property in Kamëza, though they were never allowed to reopen the school. During the Italian occupation, the army used one of their buildings as an arms depot. When Italy withdrew in 1943, a partisan band raided the depot and took the weapons. Later that year when the Germans occupied Albania, a Gestapo unit arrived at the school and, accusing them all of conspiracy with the partisans, arrested the entire family. Sevasti, then in her seventies, her sons and their wives and small children, and Paraskevi were all sent to a concentration camp near Belgrade. They managed to survive and returned to Albania in 1945 after a long and difficult journey.

When the communists came to power at the end of the Second World War, their leader, Enver Hoxha, began a ruthless and systematic purge aimed at consolidating that power. Anyone posing a threat to his authority, or even perceived as such, faced arrest. Hundreds were executed and thousands more imprisoned in the first years of communist rule. It was during this purge that Sevasti's sons were arrested and George, her youngest, eventually took his own life.

With ever increasing animosity, the religious institutions were also targeted until Hoxha finally went further than any totalitarian dictator before him when, in 1967, he proclaimed Albania 'The World's First Atheist State'. In a carefully orchestrated 'cultural revolution', 2,167 churches and mosques were either destroyed or converted into sports halls, cinemas or museums. For the next twenty-five years in Albania, simply to believe would be a punishable offence.

And so life continued until the dramatic collapse of communism in Eastern Europe at the end of the 1980s. One by one, Europe's communist regimes were swept away in a growing tide until Albania, the last to succumb, finally gave way in the spring of 1991. For the first time in fifty years, Albania's doors suddenly stood wide open to the outside world.

What followed, however, may best be described as a decade of chaos for Albania and the Balkans. The mass exodus of Albanians from Albania, the wars in Yugoslavia, the events leading to the collapse of the pyramid schemes that brought

Albania to the brink of civil war in 1997, and the Kosova crisis are sufficient proof of this fact.

Despite these tragic events, the 1990s also saw the establishment of much of what Gerasim Kyrias so diligently strived for. In the midst of much turmoil, a new Protestant community grew up at a rate that he could never have imagined.

In 1991 an umbrella organization called the Albanian Encouragement Project was formed to facilitate the efforts of the many international Protestant agencies then active throughout the country. The next year, exactly 100 years after Gerasim first founded his organization, application was made to the government to re-establish a 'Vëllazëria Ungjillore' to officially represent the needs of the emerging Protestant church. The first president of the new VUSH was Ligor Çina, one of the few Protestants from Kortcha who had survived the long years of communist suppression.

In 1996 an event took place that Gerasim would never have thought possible. The Archbishops of Albania's Catholic and Orthodox communities, together with representatives from the VUSH executive committee, joined together to form the Interconfessional Albanian Bible Society. For the first time Catholics, Orthodox, and Protestants were united in the cause of promoting the Bible in Albania.

Following over twenty years of considerable missionary activity there are today an estimated 30,000 Protestants in over 250 churches meeting across Albania. A century after his death, as a new generation of Albanians seek to bring the 'words of life' to their nation, Gerasim's vision for his people to know these words which 'enlighten hearts, bring joy and lead to the right path', is well on the way to becoming a reality.

Without the sacrifice of men and women such as those in this story, it seems unlikely Albania would ever have become a nation. And had they been allowed to freely follow their dream of educating their people and establishing Albanian schools, one can only wonder what Albania might have achieved in the century which followed, and perhaps what tragedies might have been avoided.

Gerasim's orphaned son, Stefan, as a child ca. 1900
with Athena's family. He is standing next to his uncle,
the renowned Greek preacher, Xenophon Moschou.
Courtesy of Aristotle Hadjiantoniu.

Paraskevi and Sevasti Kyrias. Courtesy of Niko Kotherja.

Appendix A

Alexander Thomson to John Baird and Edward Jenney, Monastir. Letter written in Istanbul, 2 February 1883. *ATCO*.

Dear Brethren,

The deplorable condition of the Albanian people, and especially of the Ghegs and other tribes of the nation that inhabit the country north of Berat, Monastir and Skopje up to the frontiers of Montenegro and Serbia, must be familiar to you, and has not improbably called forth your prayerful interest, though called to labour specifically for another people. With me the case is somewhat different, as my duty is to try and provide all the different nationalities of this land with the word of God, and hence I got a translation of the New Testament and Psalms executed in the Gheg dialect which where published in 1868 and 1869, and again, after the great fire of 1870, in 1872. Still much has been done for the Tosks and not without a measure of success, as is proved by the tolerably satisfactory circulation among them of the New Testament and portions of it; and of the Psalms. But among the Ghegs literally next to nothing has been done, and that chiefly from the extreme difficulty of procuring suitable agents for the work: that is, men of piety and zeal, able to speak the language of the people, and of such a position from education and otherwise as to be able in some measure to stand their ground against the arbitrary tyranny of the local authorities. In my efforts for the Ghegs I had three agents stationed in succession at Shkodra in North Albania, and something was done. But for many years I have been quite unable to find any one to station in that important city. In Skopje too, though one reason why the Bible Society regards that station with special interest is on account of the Albanian population it contains, as well as Bulgarians, nothing has been done for the former from my Agent's ignorance of the language and other reasons. I have tried also to interest missionary bodies and churches in the Albanian people, but as yet there seems little prospect of any Society or church undertaking a mission to them. In these circumstances I have resolved to make a proposal to you and to my Committee, which to me seems feasible, and on which I respectfully beg your opinion.

I wrote a short time ago to Rev. Mr. Kyrias, a preacher connected with your Mission, whom from his knowledge of both dialects of Albanian, and from his being himself an Albanian, I could not but regard as specially provided by God from the Albanian field. My object was to become acquainted with him, and to learn from him what plans he would suggest as likely to be of use in directing the Albanians to the way of life. He proposed an extensive tour to be made by him and Seefried my colporteur in Skopje, and indicated in general a deep interest in the evangelization of his nation. The tour I hold to be impracticable at present, as there is no hope of getting a Bouyourdi [sales permit] for it, at least through the British Embassy, and in view of the conditions on which Seefried was allowed to return and reside at Skopje. I acknowledge however the extreme desirableness of such a journey, and shall keep it in view as soon as there is any hope of getting permission for it.

But more important than that was the impression I received that Mr. Kyrias is every way fitted by education and zeal, specially in behalf of his own nation, to be engaged in labouring among them. Had any missionary body been prepared to undertake a Mission to the Albanians, I would have felt that it would belong to them to engage Mr. Kyrias as Missionary or evangelist, but it is otherwise. I learned some time ago from Dr. Kalopothakes of Athens, that the South Presbyterian Church of America cannot undertake an Albanian Mission, and Br[other] Baird some time ago gave me little hope that the American Board would be able or willing to do so. In these circumstances I consider I am following the directions of Providence in proposing to engage Mr. Kyrias as the Agent of the Bible Society at Shkodra in North Albania, for the general evangelization of the Albanian people, chiefly of course through the circulation of the Scriptures. He would have free liberty to preach wherever he went, he would probably have one or two colporteurs under his direction, but I would expect him himself to tour for the sale of the scriptures.

I now write to ask your opinion on this proposal, of which I shall write nothing to Mr. Kyrias till I hear from you. I trust you will see your way to sanction it. If so, I should be glad of any suggestions. Seefried cannot go to Prisrend, but Mr. Kyrias perhaps may, and if you think that or Berat preferable as the centre of the work, I may agree to it. I should also like to know what salary you would think it right to give him, allowing for his marriage, if he can find a Christian wife.

Yours most truly,
Alexander Thomson

APPENDIX B

A. Thomson to BFBS Editorial Committee, London. Written in Istanbul, 3 May 1888. *EdCI.*

The Committee are aware that the Tosk and Gheg Albanian New Testaments, and certain Books of the Old Testament were published in the Greek and Roman Alphabets respectively but accompanied with points and accents to indicate the numerous distinctive sounds of the Albanian language. I am persuaded that the course adopted so early as 1820 in the Tosk [New Testament] was a wise one. Persons of a little education, and desirous to learn the word of God, were thus enabled with a little effort to do so, but the scheme was manifestly only a temporary one, and it was easy to foresee that, if once the national spirit were called forth, and the jealousies fostered between Tosks and Ghegs by the Government were overcome, it was most desirable to have one mode of writing for the whole nation. That time seems now to have arrived, or at least to be dawning. An Albanian Committee has been formed consisting of Ghegs and Tosks, Christians and Moslems, who have devised an Alphabet which is really the Roman with the edition of some newly invented characters, and in this alphabet they have published some elementary school-books, and are continuing their labours. They have also opened at least one School in the important town of Kortcha, a day's journey from Monastir, and more Schools are in contemplation. The members of this

Committee express the utmost gratitude to the Society for having led the way in thus offering the best of all knowledge to the people in their own tongue, and desire to cooperate with us. Naturally your Agent was also desirous that this Committee should observe a favourable attitude to the Bible, and for that purpose, on the occasion of Mr. Kyrias's late visit, in November 1887, to Kortcha he authorized him to supply the School with as many copies of the Gospel of St. Matthew as were required, and they were thankfully accepted, and his whole visit was a most successful and agreeable one. That Committee now come with a request to us to publish the Gospel of Matthew and the Psalms in one of our own existing translations, but in the new Alphabet, and they promise both to use them in their Schools, and at the same time to encourage the sale among their countrymen of the Scriptures in the Greek and Roman Alphabets, which the Society has already prepared.

Appendix C

Gerasim and Sevasti Kyrias to the 1892 Annual Meeting of the European Turkey Mission. Written in Kortcha, 30 March 1892. Letter on file in the ABCFM archives, Boston. *ABC* 16.9.11.

Dear Brethren,

We heartily thank you for your deep interest in the welfare of the Albanians, and also for the material help which enabled us to open our Albanian Girls' school in this town, the only one in Albania. We opened the school with three girls, and now we have 27. They seem to be bright and promising, and are making, what seems to us, good progress. The Gospel seed is sown in the young hearts and we rejoice in seeing their gratitude for what is done for them. Some of the girls who are about 15 years old, are so eager to learn, that in order to avoid the disgrace of being seen on the street in daylight, come at dawn and remain till twilight. In a short time they have learned to write pretty fairly and read fluently. The school is opened with the reading of the Scriptures and prayer after which the girls recite the passages which each one of them has learned by heart. They are like little preachers by telling these passages to their parents and other members of their family. The work among the women looks quite encouraging. Fifteen to 20 women meet together every Friday in some house, and take a great interest in spiritual conversation. Such meetings are held in almost every quarter of the town. The number of the houses in which women's prayer meetings are held is increasing. The next two prayer meetings will be held in new places. The persecution and prejudices of the people against us are almost extinguished and friends are increasing. Many of those who have been open enemies to the truth now are friends and helpers in the work. Our Sunday school is quite interesting, as in many cases we have been compelled to prolong the lesson at the request of the hearers.

Knowing of your deep interest which you have in the conversion of these people, having shown that interest in words and deeds we take the liberty of stating before you the needs for carrying on this work, and offer to you an opportunity for rendering your benevolent services for the salvation and welfare of these neglected people. This is our humble petition:

1) One of the first things necessary is to raise native preachers and encourage those who seem fitted for the work; and if possible, one or two to be sent immediately to Albania.

2) It is very desirable that the present teacher should have an assistant teacher, as there is much work to be done, not only in the school, but also among the women, holding prayer meetings, and teaching private women to read. The number of the women who wish to learn reading has increased considerably, but the present teacher cannot find time to teach them.

3) The need of having a place for school and meetings seems to be unavoidable. It is very difficult to have it in one house, and the room which we now use for this purpose is too small. We have a sum of more than 30 liras for school and church building, 2/3 of which are contributions from friends here. We hope that when

we proceed to purchase the place some more will be collected from our friends. 100 liras, we suppose, will be sufficient for this object; and if we can get a third of the sum required from the American Board, we shall feel greatly encouraged, and will consider the enterprise as finished.

4) There is a great and growing demand for a periodical. Mr. Baird and we have made an estimation of its cost, and think that it will not be more than 100 liras, half of which, we expect to collect from subscribers. One of the friends here has promised to pay in advance for 200 copies; if the price be 15 piasters, we will get nearly 30 liras from one person. But we hope other Albanians in Egypt and Rumania will follow his example. We hope also that the London Tract Society will participate in this work. The size of it to be a little larger that the monthly *Zornitza* and to be published twice a month. We propose to have it similar in character to the 'Domasken Priatel'. The following are some of the reasons, which we think will justify our petition with regard to this periodical:

a) There is no periodical whatsoever in the Albanian language, and the people are asking our help.

b) The Albanian literature is very small, and we are sure that our paper will be read with delight and interest.

c) It will be not only the Gospel Herald all over Albania, but also the leader of the nation.

d) Moslems as well as Christians will be reached through it, especially at present, when we can hope for very few workers. A sum equal to less than one tenth of what is spent for 'Zornitza,' will cover the necessary expenses, and enable us to publish it.

These are shortly our plans, which we believe to be for the glory of our Saviour and the conversion of these people; these we bring to your consideration, in the hope that you will gladly do what can possibly be done. It should also be remembered that this is a propitious time for work in Albania, national spirit is awakening and a great demand for schools is growing. They are looking to us for help, both Moslems and Christians, and we need not say that we will try to use our influence for their spiritual good.

If you see that it will be impossible to send any missionary to Albania, we shall be very grateful if we could get half of the expenses of a missionary, with which we hope to support a native preacher and the school.

Let me say also that there are friends of the Gospel in many villages and towns in Albania, from whom we have received encouraging letters and even contributions of money for our intended church building. We have already purchased a place for a cemetery, for which we paid five Turkish liras.

Hoping that Mr. Baird in his own report will give you a fuller account about the work in Albania,

We remain

Your most obliged servants,

Gerasim D. Kyrias, Sevasti Kyrias

Appendix D

Vice-consul Howard Shipley to consul-general Blunt, Thessaloniki. Written in Monastir, 25 March 1893. *PRO FO* 294/17.

Sir,

To the objects of the above Society of Evangelists in themselves no objection can certainly be taken. Nevertheless in view of the fanaticism which is unfortunately still prevalent in these districts it may perhaps be questioned whether this new departure as an attempt to combine a religious movement with the movement which has already been on foot for some time past for the purely secular purpose of promoting the study of the Albanian language may not, at least as far as the latter are concerned, be productive of more harm than good. The originator of the new evangelical movement among the Albanians is of course Mr. Kyrias himself though he is largely aided in his efforts and especially in the educational part of his work by the American Mission at Monastir. Against Mr. Kyrias's connection with this latter mission no objection can certainly be urged though the fact of such connection will no doubt be made use of by his opponents as a proof that no spontaneous desire exists on the part of the Albanians for a spiritual revival of the kind referred to. It is however, otherwise with the question as to what extent the Society represented by Mr. Kyrias may in so far as it is endeavouring to promote an educational movement

among the Albanians also, be connected with the various
Albanian Committees or organisations abroad and particularly
with the so called Albanian Committee at Bucharest all of
which, I believe, have been formed for a similar purpose. As far
as their common object viz.: the furtherance of the study of
the Albanian language is concerned there can be no doubt that
all these Societies work together and the position taken up by
Mr. Kyrias and his friends is, I believe, that until the movement
they represent be sufficiently advanced to render itself self
supporting they are justified in accepting assistance no matter
from what quarter it may come Albanian or otherwise. I would,
however, venture to point out that however much justification
there may be for such a contention under other circumstances
there is in this case the objection that Mr. Kyrias in accepting
aid from an organisation of which the headquarters are situated
abroad can scarcely escape a share of the suspicion with which
all such organisations of the kind are undoubtedly regarded
by the Turkish Authorities. If I venture to make the above
observations it is certainly from no spirit of hostility towards
Mr. Kyrias and his friends who, personally I feel persuaded,
are only contending for the bare right of freedom to follow in
their own language their own form of religious worship, but in
order to indicate as far as possible the nature of the opposition
on which they are likely to encounter as well as the reasons of
the bitter hostility with which the movement is undoubtedly
regarded by the great majority of the more fanatical adherents
of the Greek party in southern Albania. In the meantime
whatever may be the outcome of the new movement ultimately
speaking, there can be no doubt that through its instrumentality
a most remarkable impulse has already been given to the cause

of national education in Albania. As will be seen from Mr. Kyrias's circular there are now no less than seven schools in existence in the Kortcha and Colonia districts in which Albanian and not Greek forms the basis of instruction and though the numbers of attendance where given viz.: somewhat over thirty for the girls' school (at the boys school the numbers are, I am informed, thirty-five) may appear to be small is should be borne in mind that these schools unlike those supported by the Greeks, Bulgarians and Roumanians have absolutely no extraneous endowment whatever to depend upon unless the support derived from the American Mission at Monastir and from the very precarious source of the Albanian Committee at Bucharest be excepted. It is however, an undoubtedly encouraging symptom as regards the ultimate prospects of success of the educational part of the movement that the support originally extended to it by the influential Local Beys as reported to me as far back as 1888 in my despatch No. 26 of the 5th October of that year, is still continued and, indeed, it is not too much to say that without this support the movement would never have attained the position it now occupies.

GLOSSARY

besa: (Alb.) word of honour, binding oath

bey: district chief, of lower military rank

colporteur: travelling Bible Society book-seller

Gheg: Albanian dialect spoken by Albanian tribes living north of the Shkumbi river

Grand Vizier: head of the Sublime Porte

irade: Imperial order, the 'will' of the Sultan

kaymakam: sub-governor, or chief of a district

kefil: person to stand as bail or guarantor

khan: inn

Mësonjtoria: first Albanian school opened in Kortcha in 1887

millet: (Turk. – people) term used by the Ottomans to describe a religious community

muhtar: head man, chosen one, mayor of a village

mutasarrif: district administrator, high-ranking provincial governor

opinga: leather moccasins

pasha: Ottoman honorary title for holders of political and military positions above sanjak bey

Prudential Committee: executive committee of the American Board of Commissioners for Foreign Missions based in Boston

Sublime Porte: name given to the Ottoman government

teqe: religious building used by Bektashi Muslims

Tosk: Albanian dialect spoken by Albanian tribes living south of the Shkumbi river *vali*: governor of a vilayet, or province

vilayet: Ottoman administrative province

zaptieh: policeman, gendarme

Abbreviated References
to Archival Material

ABC — The papers of the American Board of Commissioners for Foreign Missions (ABCFM) from their archives in Houghton Library, Harvard University, Boston. Shelf Marks, ABC 16.7.1, vol. 16 and 16.9, vols. 4–20 for Western Turkey, including missionaries' letters, reports, minutes, etc. Used with permission.

ATCI — Alexander Thomson's Correspondence Inward, formerly in the archives of Bible House, Istanbul. Assorted letter-books containing summarised copies of correspondence with Alexander Thomson. Used with permission.

ATCO — Alexander Thomson's Correspondence Outward, formerly in the archives of Bible House, Istanbul. Assorted letter-books containing summarised copies of Thomson's correspondence and records, reports, etc. Used with permission.

EdCI — Editorial Correspondence Inward in the archives of The British and Foreign Bible Society (BFBS), Cambridge University Library, Cambridge. Vols. 8–23. Used with permission.

EdCO — Editorial Correspondence Outward in the archives of The British and Foreign Bible Society (BFBS), Cambridge University Library, Cambridge. Vols. 8–23. Used with permission.

PRO — Public Records Office, Kew, London. Foreign Office Correspondence, *FO* 195–295, contains material relating to Gerasim's capture, problems with colportage, etc. Crown copyright. Used with permission.

NOTES

Introduction

1. Open letter from President Rexhep Mejdani to Samuel Ericsson, International Director of Advocates International, Washington, D.C. Written in Tirana, 16 February 2000.

2. Memoirs of Sevasti Kyrias/Dako (*MsDept*), type-written in Kamëza in 1936. A photocopy of one of the original versions is available at the Rare Books and Manuscripts Department in Cambridge University Library. Used with permission.

3. Dhimitër Dishnica, *Motrat Kyrias*.

4. See Hysni Myzyri, *Shkollat e para kombetare shqipe (1887–korrik 1908)*; Bedri Dedja (ed), *Gjerasim Qiriazi: Shkrime Pedagogjike; Fjalori Encyklopedik Shqiptar*; Ali Vishko, *Manastiri me rrethina në gjysmen e dytë të shekullit XIX*; etc. Like Luarasi, all contend Gerasim died a bachelor when in fact he was married and left a son. Most give his year of birth as 1861, when it was 1858.

5. *Këngë të shentëruara për falëtorët shqipe* [Sacred Songs for Albanian Churches], ed. Gjergj Kyrias, Monastir, 1906. A compilation of original hymns and translations into Albanian from English, Greek and Bulgarian.

Chapter 1

1. Stanford J. Shaw, *History of the Ottoman Empire and Modern Turkey*, vol. I, p. 281.

2. Quoted in Christo Dako, *Albania: The Master Key to the Near East*, p. 30.

3. *MsDept*, p. 17/4.

Chapter 2

1. ABCFM Annual Report, 1873, p 10.

2. 'Protestant Strength in Turkey', *The Star in the East*, 45 (January 1894), p 13.

3. William T. Stead, 'The Americanizing of Turkey', *c.* 1910. Paper on file in the archives of the American Farm School, Thessalonica, Greece. Quoted here from Marder, *Stewards of the Land*, p. 21.

4. *Missionary News, From* Bulgaria, 47 (19 March 1894), p. 1; quoted in V. Tsanoff (ed.), *Reports and Letters of American Missionaries: Referring to the Distribution of Nationalities in the Former Provinces of European Turkey, 1858–1918*, 1919.

5. E. W. Jenney to the European Turkish Mission, Annual Report for Monastir Station, 1874. Written in Monastir, 8 July 1875. *ABC* 16.9, vol. 6.

6. E. W. Jenney to ABCFM Secretary Clark. Written in Monastir, 7 March 1876. *ABC* 16.9, vol. 6.

7. E. W. Jenney to ABCFM Secretary Clark. Written in Monastir, August 1876. *ABC* 16.9, vol. 6.

8. Ibid.

9. E. W. Jenney to ABCFM Secretary Clark. Monastir, 4 January 1877. *ABC* 16.9, vol. 6.

10. A. Thomson. 'A Memoir of Mr. Kyrias, in Gerasim Kyrias, *Captured by Brigands*, trans. J. W. Baird, p. 121.

11. Ibid.

12. E. Jenney to ABCFM Secretary Clark. Written in Monastir, 4 January 1877. *ABC* 16.9, vol. 6.

13. Thomson in Kyrias, *Brigands*, p 122.

Chapter 3

1. ABCFM Annual Report, 1878, p 26.

2. ABCFM Annual Report, 1872, p 10.

3. Fred L. Kingsbury, Annual Report for Samokov College, 1881. Written in Samokov, 26 May 1882. *ABC* 16.9, vol. 7.

4. Marder, *Stewards*, p 22.

5. W. H. Belden, Annual Report for Samokov College, 1880. Written in Samokov, 10 June 1881. *ABC* 16.9, vol. 7.

6. Dako, *Master Key*, p. 89.

7. J. W. Baird, 'The First Protestant Albanian Preacher', *The Missionary Herald* (May, 1994), p. 199.

Chapter 4

1. A. Thomson to BFBS Committee, London. Written in Istanbul, 23 March 1886. Excerpt from Thomson's 25th anniversary report. *ATCO*.

2. A. Thomson to J. W. Baird, Monastir. Written in Istanbul, 28 October 1882. *ATCO*.

3. Gerasim Kyrias to A. Thomson. Written in Skopje, 15 February 1883. *ATCI*.

4. See Appendix A.

5. A. Thomson to John Sharp, London. Written in Istanbul, 7 April 1883. *ATCO*.

6. A. Thomson to Gerasim Kyrias, Skopje. Written in Istanbul, 14 April, 1883. *ATCO*.

7. Gerasim Kyrias to A. Thomson. Written in Skopje, 3 March 1883. *ATCI*.

8. Gerasim Kyrias to A. Thomson. Written in Skopje, 19 April 1883. *ATCI*.

9. A. Thomson to Gerasim Kyrias, Monastir. Written in Istanbul, 12 May 1883. *ATCO*.

10. Gerasim Kyrias to A. Thomson. Written in Kortcha, 21 May 1883. *ATCI*.

11. A. Thomson to Gerasim Kyrias, Durres. Written in Istanbul, 22 June 1883. *ATCO*.

12. A. Thomson to Gerasim Kyrias, Durres. Written in Istanbul, 29 June 1883. *ATCO*.

13. Gerasim Kyrias to A. Thomson. Written in Durres, 20 June 1883. *ATCI*.

14. A. Thomson to Gerasim Kyrias, Monastir. Written in Istanbul 6 July 1883. *ATCO*.

15. A. Thomson to Gerasim Kyrias, Monastir. Written in Istanbul 29 June 1883. *ATCO*.

16. A. Thomson to Gerasim Kyrias, Monastir. Written in Istanbul 22 August 1883. *ATCO*.

Chapter 5

1. A. Thomson to Dufferin, British ambassador in Constantinople. Written in Istanbul, 8 October 1883. *ATCO*.

2. A. Thomson to T. W. Brown, TMAS, London. Written in Istanbul, 25 February 1884. *ATCO*.

3. A. Thomson to T. W. Brown, TMAS, London. Written in Istanbul, 25 February 1884. *ATCO*.

4. A. Thomson to J. W. Baird, Monastir. Written in Istanbul, 7 March 1884. *ATCO*.

5. Shaw, *Ottoman Empire*, vol. II, p. 219.

6. A. Thomson to T.W. Brown, TMAS, London. Written in Istanbul, 12 April 1884. *ATCO*.

7. A. Thomson to BFBS Secretary Chas. E. B. Reed, London. Written in Istanbul, 5 April 1884. *ATCO*.

8. A. Thomson to BFBS Secretary Chas. E. B. Reed, London. Written in Istanbul, 8 April 1884. *ATCO*.

Chapter 6

1. A. Thomson's Annual Report for 1884 to the BFBS Committee, London. Written in Istanbul during January–February 1885. *ATCO*.

2. Quoted in Skender Luarasi, *Gjerasim Qiriazi, Jeta dhe Vepra*, p 26.

3. A. Thomson's Annual Report for 1884 to the BFBS Committee, London. Written in Istanbul. *ATCO*.

4. A. Thomson article in *The Star in the East*, 9 (January 1885). Periodical of the TMAS published in London by James Nesbit & Co.

5. Luarasi, *Gjerasim Qiriazi*, p. 27.

6. *MsDept*, p. 11.

7. Luarasi, *Gjerasim Qiriazi*, pp. 23-24.

8. L. Bond to British Embassy in Istanbul. Written in Monastir, 15 November 1884. Letter on file at the Public Records Office (*PRO*), London. *FO 195/1485*.

9. A. Thomson to Rev. J. Sharp M. A., London. Written in Istanbul, 29 November 1884. *ATCO*.

10. J. E. Blunt to British Embassy, Istanbul. Written in Thessaloniki, 18 November 1884. *PRO FO 295/6*.

11. A. Thomson to Rev. J. Sharp M. A., London. Written in Istanbul, 29 November 1884. *ATCO*.

12. The author was told by Shahin Matraku's aged niece during a visit to his home village of Popqishta in 1997, that he and two of his men had been invited by their betrayers to a special feast in a Bektashi teqe high in the mountains. During the meal, Turkish soldiers surrounded the building. Inside, one of Shahin's friends challenged him to a show of strength for sport and pinned Shahin's arms behind his back. The soldiers then rushed in and overpowered Shahin and his two men. They cut off their heads, which were sent to Monastir and set out for public display. Estimated date of Shahin's death is around 1890.

13. J. E. Blunt to British Embassy, Istanbul. Written in Thessaloniki, 14 March 1885. *PRO FO 295/6*.

14. Ibid.

15. A. Thomson to Hugh Wyndham, British Chargé d'Affaires, Istanbul. Written in Istanbul, 3 March 1885. *ATCO*.

16. A. Thomson to Rev. T. W. Brown, TMAS, London. Written in Istanbul, 6 March 1885. *ATCO*.

17. J. E. Blunt to British Embassy in Istanbul. Written in Thessaloniki, 4 March 1885. *PRO FO 195/515*.

18. J. E. Blunt to British Embassy in Istanbul. Written in Thessaloniki, 10 March 1885. *PRO FO 195/515*.

19. J. E. Blunt to British Embassy in Istanbul. Written in Thessaloniki, 11 April 1885. *PRO FO 195/515*.

20. J. E. Blunt to British Embassy in Istanbul. Thessaloniki, 11 April 1885. *PRO FO 295/6*.

21. J. E. Blunt to British Embassy in Istanbul. Written in Thessaloniki, 22 April 1885. *PRO FO 195/515*.

22. Kyrias, *Brigands*, p. 97.

23. *MsDept*, p. 87.

24. Kyrias, *Brigands*, p. 124.

Chapter 7

1. Gerasim Kyrias, report in *The Star in the East*, 14 (April, 1886), p. 16.

2. A. Thomson to BFBS Committee, London. 1887 Annual Report. Written in Istanbul during January–February 1888. *ATCO*.

3. A. Thomson to Thomas W. Brown, TMAS, London. Written in Istanbul, 10 November 1885. *ATCO*.

4. Gerasim Kyrias, report in *The Star in the East*, 14 (April, 1886), p. 15.

5. Gerasim Kyrias, *Letra e Vëllazërisë*, 1 (1892) Published by the Vëllazëria Ungjillore e Korçës, Kortcha. On file at the Albanian State Archives, Tirana.

6. A. Thomson to Gerasim Kyrias, Monastir. Written in Istanbul, 14 April 1886. *ATCO*.

7. A. Thomson to Gerasim Kyrias, Monastir. Written in Istanbul, 18 August 1886. *ATCO*.

8. A. Thomson to BFBS Committee, London. 1886 Annual Report. Written in Istanbul during January–February 1887. *ATCO*.

9. Ibid.

10. Ibid.

11. Ibid.

12. A. Thomson to Gerasim Kyrias, Monastir. Written in Istanbul, 2 July 1887. *ATCO*.

13. A. Thomson to T. W. Brown, TMAS, London. Written in Istanbul, 16 March 1888. *ATCO*.

14. A. Thomson to Gerasim Kyrias, Monastir. Written in Istanbul, 14 December 1887. *ATCO*.

15. A. Thomson to Gerasim Kyrias, Monastir. Written in Istanbul, 31 December 1887. *ATCO*.

16. *MsDept*, p. 51.

17. See Appendix B.

18. A. Thomson to BFBS Committee, London. Annual Report, 1889. Written in Istanbul during January–February 1890. *ATCO*.

19. Vice-consul H. Shipley to J. E. Blunt. Written in Monastir, 20 August 1888. *PRO FO* 195/1619.

20. A. Thomson to BFBS Committee, London. Annual Report, 1889. Written in Istanbul during January–February 1890. *ATCO*.

21. Ibid.

22. Ibid.

23. J. E. Blunt to ambassador White, British Embassy in Istanbul. Written in Thessaloniki, 23 August 1888. *PRO FO* 195/1619.

24. A. Thomson to H. M. ambassador Francis Clare Ford. Written in Istanbul in February 1889. *ATCO*.

25. A. Thomson to BFBS Committee, London. Written in Istanbul on 4 May 1889. *EdCI*.

26. Luarasi, *Gjerasim Qiriazi*, p. 45.

27. A. Thomson to Gerasim Kyrias, Monastir. Written in Istanbul, 6 November 1889. *ATCO*.

28. H. Shipley to J. E. Blunt, Thessaloniki. Written in Monastir, 6 October, 1889. *PRO FO* 195/1655.

29. Gerasim Kyrias to A. Thomson. Written in Monastir, 19 November 1889. *ATCI*.

30. Gerasim Kyrias to A. Thomson. Written in Athens, 17 December 1889. *ATCI*.

31. Gerasim Kyrias to A. Thomson. Written in Shkodra, 23 December 1889. *ATCI*.

32. Gerasim Kyrias to A. Thomson. Written in Shkodra, 27 December 1889. *ATCI*.

33. Luarasi, *Gerasim Kyrias*, p. 51.

Chapter 8

1. J. E. Blunt to H. M. ambassador White. Written in Thessaloniki, 3 April 1890. *PRO FO* 195/169.

2. Gerasim Kyrias to A. Thomson, Istanbul. Written in Vlora, 5 March 1890. *ATCI*.

3. Gerasim Kyrias to A. Thomson, Istanbul. Written in Shkodra, 9 January 1890. *ATCI*.

4. A. Thomson to BFBS Committee, London. 1890 Annual Report. Written in Istanbul during January–February, 1891. *ATCO*.

Chapter 9

1. Gerasim Kyrias to A. Thomson. Written in Kortcha, 8 May 1890. *ATCI*.

2. Gerasim Kyrias to A. Thomson. Written in Kortcha, 12 May 1890. *ATCI*.

3. Ibid.

4. Ibid.

5. A. Thomson to Gerasim Kyrias, Kortcha. Written in Istanbul, 31 May 1990. *ATCO*.

6. Ibid.

7. A. Thomson to Gerasim Kyrias, Kortcha. Written in Istanbul, 10 June 1990. *ATCO*.

8. A. Thomson to Gerasim Kyrias, Kortcha. Written in Istanbul, 31 July 1990. *ATCO*.

9. A. Thomson to Gerasim Kyrias, Kortcha. Written in Istanbul, 13 November 1990. *ATCO*.

10. Myzyri, *Shkollat e para*, p. 94.

11. Ibid., p. 92.

12. A. Thomson to Gerasim Kyrias, Monastir. Written in Istanbul, 14 February 1991. *ATCO*.

13. A. Thomson to Gerasim Kyrias, Kortcha. Written in Istanbul, 11 April 1991. *ATCO*.

14. A. Thomson to Gerasim Kyrias, Kortcha. Written in Istanbul, 4 April 1991. *ATCO*.

Chapter 10

1. Carrie Borden, 'Constantinople Home', undated handwritten report. *ABC* 16.7.1, vol. 16.

2. *MsDept*, p. 20.

3. Ibid., pp. 58–62.

4. Carrie Borden. Report on Commencement Week of the American College for Girls at Constantinople, June 1891. *ABC* 16.7.1, vol. 16.

5. *MsDept*.

6. A. Thomson to George Kyrias, Shkodra. Written in Istanbul, 17 August 1891. *ATCO*.

7. A. Thomson to George Kyrias, Thessaloniki. Written in Istanbul, 2 September 1891. *ATCO*.

8. A. Thomson to BFBS Secretary Paull, London. Written in Istanbul, 1891, exact date unknown. *ATCO*.

9. J. Baird to ABCFM Secretary Clark, Boston. Written in Monastir, 14 October 1891. *ABC* 16.9, vol. 11.

10. J. W. Baird to ABCFM Secretary Clark, Boston. Written in Monastir, 22 November 1891. *ABC* 16.9, vol. 11.

11. *MsDept*, p. 65.

12. Ibid., pp. 68–9.

13. Ibid.

14. J. W. Baird to ABCFM Secretary Clark, Boston. Written in Monastir, 14 October 1891. *ABC* 16.9, vol. 11.

15. Sevasti Kyrias, 'Fjalë', in *Hristomaci*, ed. Gjergj Kyrias, pp. 319–20.

16. Ibid., p. 321.

17. J. W. Baird to ABCFM Secretary Clark, Boston. Written in Monastir, 17 December 1891. *ABC* 16.9, vol. 11.

Chapter 11

1. A. Thomson to Bosdoyannes, Yanina. Written in Istanbul, 28 December 1891. *ATCO*.

2. A. Thomson to Secretary Paull, London. Written in Istanbul, 21 October 1891. *ATCO*.

3. A. Thomson to Gerasim Kyrias, Kortcha. Written in Istanbul, 28 October 1891. *ATCO*.

4. A. Thomson to Gerasim Kyrias, Kortcha. Written in Istanbul, 14 November 1891. *ATCO*.

5. A. Thomson to Gerasim Kyrias, Monastir. Written in Istanbul, 1 February 1892. *ATCO*.

6. A. Thomson to Gerasim Kyrias, Kortcha. Written in Istanbul, 19 March 1892. *ATCO*.

7. A. Thomson to Secretary Paull, London. Written in Istanbul, 30 January 1892. *ATCO*.

8. J. Baird to ABCFM Secretary Clark, Boston. Written in Kortcha, 20 February 1892. *ABC* 16.9, vol. 11.

9. Ibid.

10. See Appendix C

11. A. Thomson to Gerasim Kyrias, Kortcha. Written in Istanbul, 23 April 1892. *ATCO*.

12. A. Thomson to Gerasim Kyrias, Kortcha. Written in Istanbul, 2 April 1892. *ATCO*.

13. A. Thomson to J. Baird, Monastir. Written in Istanbul, 23 March 1892. *ATCO*.

14. A. Thomson to Gerasim Kyrias, Kortcha. Written in Istanbul 2 April 1892. *ATCO*.

15. A. Thomson to Gerasim Kyrias, Kortcha. Written in Istanbul 12 May 1892. *ATCO*.

16. A. Thomson to Gerasim Kyrias, Kortcha. Written in Istanbul 6 May 1892. *ATCO*.

17. A. Thomson to Gerasim Kyrias, Kortcha. Written in Istanbul 14 May 1892. *ATCO*.

18. A. Thomson to H.M. ambassador F.C. Ford, Istanbul. Written in Istanbul, 27 April 1892. *ATCO*.

19. H. Shipley to J. E. Blunt, Thessaloniki. Written in Monastir, 12 August 1891. *PRO FO* 294/17.

20. A. Thomson to Gerasim Kyrias, Kortcha. Written in Istanbul, 6 June 1892. *ATCO*

21. A. Thomson to Gerasim Kyrias, Thessaloniki. Written in Istanbul, 16 August 1892. *ATCO*.

22. H. Shipley to J. E. Blunt, Thessaloniki. Letter incorrectly dated as 20 January 1892, actually written 1893.

Shipley's letter forwarded by Blunt to H.M. Embassy in Istanbul, 25 March 1893. *FO 294/17*.

23. N. N. Naço to A. Thomson. Written in Bucharest, 18 February 1893. *ATCI*.

24. A. Thomson to Gerasim Kyrias, Kortcha. Written in Istanbul, 5 August 1892. *ATCO*.

25. A. Thomson to H. M. ambassador F. C. Ford, Istanbul. Written in Istanbul, May 1893. *ATCO*.

26. *MsDept*.

27. J. W. Baird. Report from Kortcha dated 20 October 1892. *Missionary News* (December, 1892), p. 2.

28. Ibid., p. 3.

29. Ibid.

Chapter 12

1. Kalopothakes to A. Thomson, Istanbul. Written in Athens, 9 October 1892. *ATCI*.

2. A. Thomson to Gerasim Kyrias, Kortcha. Written in Istanbul, 5 November 1892. *ATCO*.

3. Gerasim Kyrias to A. Thomson, Istanbul. Written in Kortcha, 16 November 1892. *ATCI*.

4. J. W. Baird to ABCFM Secretary Clark, Boston. Written in Monastir, 16 November 1892. *ABC* 16.9, vol. 11.

5. H. Shipley to J. E. Blunt. Written in Monastir, November 1892. *PRO FO 195/1802*.

6. Gerasim Kyrias to A. Thomson, Istanbul. Written in Kortcha, 16 November 1892. *ATCI*.

7. J. W. Baird to ABCFM Secretary Clark, Boston. Written in Monastir, 28 December, 1892. *ABC* 16.9, vol. 11.

8. J. W. Baird to ABCFM Secretary Clark, Boston. Written in Monastir, 16 November 1892. *ABC* 16.9, vol. 11.

9. Gerasim Kyrias to A. Thomson, Istanbul. Written in Kortcha, 16 November 1892. *ATCI.*

10. Ibid.

11. See Appendix D.

12. J. E. Blunt to H. M. Embassy, Istanbul. Written in Thessaloniki, 8 April, 1893. *PRO FO* 195/1802.

13. Ibid.

14. Gerasim Kyrias to A. Thomson, Istanbul. Written in Kortcha, 14 December 1892. *ATCI.*

15. Gerasim Kyrias to A. Thomson, Istanbul. Written in Kortcha, 11 November 1892. *ATCI.*

16. Gerasim Kyrias to A. Thomson, Istanbul. Written in Kortcha, 21 December 1892. *ATCI.*

17. Gerasim Kyrias to A. Thomson, Istanbul. Written in Kortcha, 10 January 1893. *ATCI.*

18. Ibid.

19. A. Thomson to Gerasim Kyrias, Kortcha. Written in Istanbul, 5 November 1892. *ATCO.*

20. Gerasim Kyrias to A. Thomson, Istanbul. Written in Kortcha, 18 January 1893. *ATCI.*

21. Ibid.

22. *MsDept.*

23. Gerasim Kyrias to A. Thomson, Istanbul. Written in Kortcha, 28 January, 1893. *ATCI.*

24. Ibid.

25. Gerasim Kyrias to A. Thomson, Istanbul. Written in Kortcha, 18 January, 1893. *ATCI.*

26. Ibid.

27. A. Thomson to H. M. ambassador C. Ford. Written in Istanbul, February 1893. *ATCO*.

28. Gerasim Kyrias to A. Thomson, Istanbul. Written in Kortcha, 28 January 1893. *ATCI*.

29. Gerasim Kyrias to A. Thomson, Istanbul. Written in Kortcha, 31 January 1893. *ATCI*.

30. Gerasim Kyrias to A. Thomson, Istanbul. Written in Kortcha, 21 February 1893. *ATCI*.

Chapter 13

1. Gerasim Kyrias to A. Thomson, Istanbul. Written in Kortcha, 21 February 1893. *ATCI*.

2. Gerasim Kyrias, 'E para ditë e majit', in *Hristomaci*, p. 82.

3. *MsDept*.

4. Gerasim Kyrias to A. Thomson, Istanbul. Written in Kortcha, 21 February 1893. *ATCI*.

5. Ibid.

6. A. Thomson to BFBS Secretary Paull, London. Written in Istanbul, 8 April 1893. *ATCO*.

7. H. Shipley to A. Thomson, Istanbul. Written in Monastir, 27 June 1893. *ATCI*.

Chapter 14

1. *MsDept*, pp. 75–6.

2. Ibid., p. 76.

3. A. Thomson to Sevasti Kyrias, Monastir. Written in Istanbul, 3 January 1894. *ATCO*.

4. Dako, *Master Key*, p. 86.

5. *MsDept*.

6. J. W. Baird, 'The First Protestant Albanian Preacher', *Missionary Herald* (May 1894), p. 200.

7. Gerasim Kyrias, 'Lamtumirë, *Ylli i Mëngjesit*, 3:7 (November 1918), p. 29.

Epilogue

1. Michal Grameno, *Kryengritje Shqiptare* [Albanian Uprisings], 1925, pp. 43–4.

2. Dako, *Master Key*, p. 89.

3. Midhat Bey Frashëri, 'Albania and the Bible Society', *The Bible and the World* (July, 1912), p. 218.

BIBLIOGRAPHY

Agapidis, Ioannis, *Suntomos istoria* [History of the Evangelical Church in Thessaloniki] (Thessaloniki: Presbyter of the Greek Evangelical Church of Thessaloniki, 1953).

Baird, John W., 'The First Protestant Albanian Preacher', *The Missionary Herald* (1849-1940) Periodical of the ABCFM, Boston, May, 1894.

Barton, James L., 'Free Albania: A Momentous Situation Confronting the American Board' (Boston: ABCFM, 1914).

Bland, W. H., *Albania* (Oxford: The Orleander Press, 1987).

Buda, Aleks (ed.), *Historia e popullit shqiptar*, vol. II (Tirana: Universiteti Shtetëror i Tiranës, Instituti i Historisë dhe Gjuhësisë, 1965).

Buda, Aleks, et al. (eds), *Fjalori Encyklopedik Shqiptar* [The Albanian Encyclopedia] (Tirana: Kombinati Poligrafik Shtypëshkronja e Re, 1985).

Byron, Lord George Gordon, *The Poems and Dramas of Lord Byron*, 2 vols. (Chicago: Belford-Clarke Co., 1891).

Canton, William. *A History of the British and Foreign Bible Society*, 5 vols. (London: John Murray, 1904–1910).

Castellan, Georges, *Histori e Ballkanit* [History of the Balkans], trans. into Albanian from French (Tirana: Çabej MÇM, 1996).

Dako, Christo, *Albania: the Master Key to the Middle East* (Boston: E.L. Grimes Co., 1919).

_____, *Cilët janë Shqipëtarët?* [Who are the Albanians?] (Monastir: Shtypshkronja Tregëtare Ndërkombëtare, 1911).

Dedja, Bedri (ed.), *Gerasim Kyrias: Shkrime Pedagogjike* (Tirana: Biblioteka Pedagogjike, 1966).

Dërmaku, Ismet. *Rilindja Kombëtare shqiptare dhe kolonitë shqiptarë të mërgimit në Rumani dhe në Bullgari* (Prishtina: Enti i Teksteve dhe i Mjeteve Mësimore i Krahines Socialiste Autonome të Kosovës, 1990).

Dishnica, Dhimitër, *Motrat Kyrias* (Tirana: Shtëpia Botuese 'Enciklopedike', 1997).

Durham, Edith. *Burden of the Balkans* (London: Thomson Nelson & Sons, 1905).

_____, *High Albania* (London: Edward Arnold, 1909).

Frashëri, Midhat Bey, 'The Development of Albania', *The Bible in the World* [monthly magazine of the BFBS] (London: Hazell, Watson & Viney, October, 1911).

_____, 'Albania and the Bible Society', *The Bible in the World* (London: Hazell, Watson & Viney, July, 1912).

Grameno, Michal, *Kryengritje Shqiptare* [Albanian Uprisings] (Vlora: Shtypëshkronja Vlora, 1925).

Grigoriatis, Damaskinos, *Protestantet Heretike* [The Heretical Protestants] (Thessaloniki: Bashkimi Orthodhox Kristian 'Kryqi i nderuar' Publishing House, 1996).

Hadri, Ali (ed.), *Lidha Shqiptare e Prizrenit në Dokumente Angleze* [The Albanian League in the English Documents] (Prishtina: Arkivi i Kosovës, 1978).

Jacques, Edwin, *The Albanians, An Ethnic History from Pre-historic Times to the Present* (Jefferson, N.C.: McFarland and Company, Inc.,1995).

Janura, Petro. *Nga historia e alfabetit të gjuhës shqipe* [From the History of the Albanian Alphabet] (Skopje: NIP Nova Makedonia, 1969).

Karanxha, Ilia, 'Do të punoj për mëmëdhe, gjithë jetën sa të rronj' [I Will Work for the Motherland my Whole Life, as Long as I Live], *Mësuesi* (Tirana: 25 October, 1988).

Latourette, Kenneth, *History of Christianity* (New York: Harper & Brothers, 1953).

Lloshi, Xhevat, 'Të dhëna dokumentare të reja mbi veprimtarisë e V. Meksit, G. Gjirokastritit dhe K. Kristoforidhit' ['New Documentary Evidence Concerning the Work of V. Meksi, G. Gjiokastriti and K. Kristoforidhi'], *Studime Filologjike 3* (1973).

Luarasi, Skender, *Gjerasim Qiriazi, Jeta dhe Vepra* [Gerasim Kyrias, Life and Writings] (Tirana: Naim Frashëri, 1962).

_____, *Petro Luarasi, Jeta dhe Vepra* (Tirana: Naim Frashëri, 1958).

Marder, Brenda L., *Stewards of the Land* (Boulder: East European Quarterly, 1979).

Miller, William, *The Ottoman Empire and its Successors* (London, Frank Cass & Co. Ltd., 1966).

Mojzes, Paul Benjamin, *A History of the Congregational and Methodist Churches in Bulgaria and Yugoslavia.* Unpublished Ph.D. dissertation, Boston University, 1965.

Myzyri, Hysniu, *Shkollat e para kombetare shqipe (1887-korrik 1908)* [The First National Albanian Schools (1887-July 1908)] (Tirana: 8 Nëntori Publishing House, 1978).

_____, *Nuçi Naçi* (Tirana: Librat Shkollor Publishing House, 1986).

_____, *100-vjetori i mësonjëtores së parë shqipe në Korçë* [The 100th Anniversary of the First Albanian School in Kortcha], eds. Luan Hajdaraga, et al. (Tirana: Librat Shkollor Publishing House, 1987).

Myzyri, Hysniu (ed.), *Historia e popullit shqiptar, për shkollat e mesme* [The History of the Albanian People, for Middle Schools] (Tirana: Libri shkollor Publishing House, 1994).

Osmani, Tomor, *Histori e alfabetit të gjuhës shqipe* [The History of the Alphabet of the Albanian Language] (Tirana: Librit Shkollor Publishing House, 1987).

Piraku, Muhamet. *Kultura kombëtare shqiptare* [The Culture of the Albanian People] (Prishtina: Instituti Albanologjik i Prishtinës, 1989).

Protestantet janë orthodokse të parë (Qemoçme) Cilët janë Protestantët [The Protestants are the first Orthodox] (Kortcha: Dhori Koti, 1931).

Kyrias, Gerasim, 'Released from Captivity', *Gleanings for the Young*. Publication of the BFBS (London: November, 1885), 129–30.

_____, article in *The Star in the East*, 14 (April 1886), 15–6.

_____, *Letra e Vëllazerisë* (Kortcha: Vëllazëria Ungjillore e Korçës, 1892–3).

_____, *Psalmet*. Revision of K. Kristoforidhi's translation of the Psalms in Tosk Albanian. Transcribed by A. Sina, 1895. Manuscript on file in the BFBS archives, Cambridge.

_____, *Captured by Brigands*, trans. by J. W. Baird (London: Religious Tract Society, c. 1902).

_____, *Hristomadhi*. In four parts containing original and translated material by Gerasim Kyrias as well as Sevasti and Gjergj. Ed. Gjergj Kyrias (Sophia: Shtypëshkronja 'Mbrothësia', 1902).

_____, 'Lamtumirë', *Yll' i mëngjesit*. Albanian periodical published 1917–19, ed. Paraskevi Kyrias. Boston.

_____, *Këngë të shentëruara për falëtorët shqipe* [Sacred Songs for Albanian Churches] Compilation of original hymns and translations into Albanian from English, Greek and Bulgarian. Ed. Gjergj Qiriaz. First published in Monastir, 1906. Reprinted in Kortcha: Dhori Koti, 1927.

Kyrias, Sevasti, 'Fjalë', in *Hristomaci*, ed. Gjergj Kyrias (Sofia: n.p., 1902).

Reid, Daniel G., et al. (eds.), *Dictionary of Christianity in America* (Downers Grove, Illinois: IVP, 1990).

Shaw, Stanford, J., *History of the Ottoman Empire and Modern Turkey* 2 vols. (Cambridge: Cambridge University Press, 1976)

Shuteriqi, Dhimitër, *Naim Frasheri* (Tirana: 8 Nëntori Publishing House, 1982).

Skendi, Stavro, *The Albanian National Awakening 1878–1918* (Princeton: Princeton University Press, 1967).

Tako, Piro, 'Një libër të panjohur' ['An unknown book'], article about the discovery of Kyrias's book, *Captured by Brigands*, *Drita* (11 January 1987).

Thomson, Alexander, 'A Memoir of Mr Kyrias's, *Captured by Brigands* (London: Religious Tract Society, c. 1902).

Tsanoff, Vladimir A. (ed.), *Report and Letters of American Missionaries: Referring to the distribution of Nationalities in the Former Provinces of European Turkey, 1858–1918* (Sofia: n.p., 1919).

Veronis, Luke A., *Missionaries, Monks and Martyrs: Making Disciples of All Nations* (Minneapolis: Light and Life Publishing, 1994).

Vishko, Ali, *Manastiri me rrethina në gysmen e dytë të shekullit XIX* [Monastir and its Environs During the Second Half of the 19th Century] (Skopje: Flaka e Vëllazërimit Publishers, 1988).

Ware, Timothy, *The Orthodox Church* (New York: Penguin Books, 1963).

INDEX

INSTITUTE *for* ALBANIAN *&* PROTESTANT STUDIES

The mission of the Institute for Albanian and Protestant Studies is to promote the discovery of Albanian and Protestant history and thought.

This book is part of the 500/200 Series published in commemoration of the 500th anniversary of the Protestant Reformation in Europe, the 200th anniversary of the Albanian Bible translation project, the 150th anniversary of the publication of the Gheg Albanian Gospels, and the 125th anniversaries of the Albanian Evangelical Brotherhood and the Albanian Girls' School in Kortcha. The titles in this series include:

- *My Life: the autobiography of the pioneer of female education in Albania, Sevasti Kyrias Dako*

- *Gerasim Kyrias and the Albanian National Awakening, 1858–1894* (John Quanrud)

- *Captured by Brigands* (Gerasim Kyrias)

- *Albania and the Albanians in the Annual Reports of the British and Foreign Bible Society*

- *Albania and the Albanians in the Annual Reports of the American Board of Commissioners for Foreign Missions*

- *Travels in Albania, Selected Writings from British Authoresses, 1717–1878*

www.instituti.org

Made in United States
Orlando, FL
05 March 2024

44405805R00168